Miniatures

Published by BEAM Education

Copyright © BEAM 2000

Note

The Early Learning Goals listed in the chart on p106 are from the

QCA (Qualifications and Curriculum Authority) document

Early Learning Goals, © Qualifications and Curriculum Authority 1999

All rights reserved

ISBN 1 874099 64 2

Illustrated by Kelly Dooley

Designed and typeset by BEAM Education

Printed in England by Print-source

British Library Cataloguing-in-Publication Data

A catalogue record for this publication is available

from the British Library

Contents

Introduction

MiniMaths is packed with ideas for mathematical activity with young children. It is a resource for adults working with Nursery, Reception or pre-school children in any early years setting.

Each chapter uses an 'everyday' item such as our hands, or containers, as the basis for a wide range of mathematical activity. This approach has three significant benefits:

- it de-mystifies maths by showing that mathematical activity can make use of whatever is to hand

- it makes clear to children that mathematics is inherent in our everyday practical lives: at home, at school and in the world around us

- it makes use of familiar items to tackle less familiar mathematical ideas

How do children learn?

Mathematical activity needs to take account of the interests and enthusiasms of young children. Children have a natural curiosity in what is around them, and this includes the mathematical. By cutting, drawing, handling items and playing games, young children demonstrate their willingness to become involved in mathematics.

Young children learn through:

- **Play** Children need the opportunity to take control of mathematics in the context of play. Playing with ideas helps children develop the confidence to 'have a go' — and to learn when and where to go for help if necessary.

- **Repetition** Frequent repetition of an enjoyable activity makes it familiar to children, giving a sense of control over the mathematics involved.

- **Communication** Children learn through doing things with others, and in particular by talking to each other and to adults about what is taking place at each stage of an activity. Talk is the link between doing something and knowing something.

- **Observation** It is important to give children the opportunity to watch and listen, both to adults and to each other. It is as appropriate to watch and listen in mathematics as it is in other curriculum areas. When we watch and listen we have opportunities to observe differences and similarities, to share ideas and to use other people's ideas to build on our own.

- **Practical contexts** Mathematics is a mental activity — but mental work must be based on practical activity. Children's mental strategies need to be developed in a variety of contexts that can be 'seen' and visualised.

What children learn at home and school

All young children arrive at their early years setting with a wealth of mathematical knowledge from home that they will bring to bear on their new learning experiences. Future learning has to take account of this knowledge. Talk to families and carers about the maths you and the children are doing, so that they can support their child's mathematics learning at home. Include families and carers by asking them to help collect appropriate resources (egg boxes, cereal packets and so on), or by inviting them to come in and participate in activities. Carers will get a clear picture of the maths their children do in school if they can come in and talk to you and to the children, listen to the songs you sing, and hear the discussions you have and the questions you ask. All of this opens up a mathematical dialogue between children, families and schools.

The Early Learning Goals (QCA, DfEE,1999) define aims for all children at the end of their Reception year. Nursery and Reception teachers will have the Early Learning Goals in mind as an end point and will plan with regard to the development of the 'whole child'. *MiniMaths* is cross-referenced both to the Early Learning Goals themselves (see the chart on p106), and to significant steps leading up to the Goals (see the chart at the end of each chapter). This is to support you in the planning and assessment of the activities.

Background theory to MiniMaths

MiniMaths is based on a 'talk, do, talk, do again, talk' cycle. It provides:

- structured activities to either precipitate or follow free play, for children to explore and reinforce their own ideas and their own learning
- plenty of opportunities for children to talk about what they are going to do, what they are doing and what they have done

MiniMaths recognises that young children need to learn both to focus on a task alone and to work with others. Some activities begin with children pooling ideas about how to go about something before they work alone, and end with children sharing their results with each other. Others involve children working cooperatively as part of a small group, for example when playing a game.

All the activities are structured around 'open' questions such as: "How can you...?", "How might we...?", "How will you...?". Discussing and solving problems lies at the heart of *MiniMaths*, just as problem-solving lies at the heart of mathematics.

MiniMaths prioritises practical and mental work. Children only make records of their work on paper as an integral part of a task. You might, for example, ask: "How can you remember that?", "Can you show all the combinations you have found?" or "Can you think of a way of keeping track on paper of the ones you have found?"

Ways to introduce MiniMaths

You might choose to spend a week using, say, 'Green Peppers' as the focal point for your mathematics. Each chapter opens with 'all together', ideas for preliminary activities, 'Let's Sing', 'Let's Do' and 'Let's Investigate', to introduce the topic. The twelve activities in each chapter cover a broad range of mathematics. In the margins you will find lists of the key vocabulary and the maths learning covered, and the significant steps chart at the end of each chapter provides a more detailed guide to the mathematical content of the activities. Finally, you can match the content of each activity to the Early Learning Goals at a glance by referring to the table on p106.

Each activity can be chosen as it stands for a group of children to do initially with an adult. The activity can then be left out for children to explore in their free play. Alternatively, some of the more structured activities, such as games, might be more successful when preceded by free play with the resources. To ensure that children get the maximum benefit from the activities, you will need to provide opportunities for them to repeat the tasks, either alone in their play or as part of a group. You can also adapt tasks for children to take home and share with their families and carers. Each activity includes two 'challenges' for the most interested children.

The 'Can the child…' section in each activity lists the assessment points for each activity. It refers not only to mathematics goals, but to the young child's personal, social and emotional development.

Dip in and enjoy your *MiniMaths*!

How to use this book

MiniMaths is divided into six chapters. Each chapter contains twelve activities covering a range of mathematical experiences.

The activities can be used flexibly to accommodate the requirements of Nursery or Reception children. Each activity offers challenges, which can be used as extensions for older or more able children.

At the end of each chapter is a chart showing significant steps that we have identified for early years learning. Finally, on p106 you will find a table linking every activity in the book to the QCA's Early Learning Goals.

All sorts

Ask the children to sort out the bears, according to different criteria. For instance, explain that only bears with outdoor clothing can play outside, or only small bears can ride in the cart. Invite the children to think of and draw a label for each set.

Things to ask

- Are all these bears similar in some way?
- What is the same about this group of bears?
- Why does this bear not go in this set?
- What does your label tell us about these bears?

Challenges

Hide the label for a set. The children decide what the bears have in common and write a new label for the set.

Children make another set using different objects.

Can the child...

Sort the bears according to the criteria suggested.

Say why a particular bear does or does not belong to a particular group.

Think of and draw a label to describe a set.

Initiate ideas and talk about what he is doing.

Teddy bears

You will need

- a large collection of different teddy bears
- drawing paper or card
- felt-tipped pens
- luggage labels

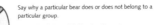

sort
group
set
compare
size
long
short
tall
pick out
wide
pick out

Maths learning

Use developing mathematical ideas and methods to solve practical problems.
Use language to compare two quantities.
Use language to describe the shape and size of solids and flat shapes.

45

You will need

This lists the resources you will need to provide for the activity.

Key words

These are words you will probably use naturally during the activity. Most of the words are listed in the NNS *Mathematical Vocabulary* book. Others are everyday words used in a mathematical context. For some activities, you may like the children to repeat and use the words themselves; for others, you may choose just to introduce the vocabulary, giving it in a range of contexts for a good understanding.

Things to ask

This gives some ideas for questions to ask, to stimulate the children's thought processes and encourage the use of mathematical vocabulary. Most of the suggestions are 'open' questions, to encourage exploration and develop self-confidence. The questioning might also be used to support children with specific needs.

Challenges

These are suggestions for ways to extend or vary the activity for older or more able children.

Maths learning

This section gives you an 'at-a-glance' guide to the mathematics covered in each activity. For a more in-depth guide, please see the Early Learning Goals chart at the end of the book.

Can the child...

This is an assessment checklist for practitioners. It gives you an idea of what to look out for when assessing the children's mathematical understanding and personal and social development.

Hands

This chapter explores how we can do maths with our hands. We might use hands to count, either on our fingers or by clapping, or as tools to measure length. We can investigate size, quantity and weight by seeing how much our hands can hold, or how many objects we can feel. We can also use touch to find out the shapes and properties of objects. Pairs, and simple patterns of left and right, arise naturally when working with hands.

Contents

Hands

Let's sing

"Five little speckled frogs sat on a speckled log..."

Sing the song using your fingers to represent the frogs.

Sing the song again using children as the frogs. The five 'frogs' can hold number cards, and jump off the 'log' in order.

What else could we use to sing this song? Finger puppets?

"If you're happy and you know it clap your hands..."

Sing the song, introducing a different way of using your hands each time: shaking hands, pointing fingers…

How many different ways can we think of?

How can we remember them? Could we draw them?

Let's do

Count up to large numbers

Keep the rhythm of counting by clapping hands, pointing or tapping knees.

One, TWO, three, FOUR, five, SIX…

"All hold hands and make a line, a circle, a triangle"

Draw shapes in chalk on the floor for the children to stand on.

What is this shape called?

What other shapes can we make?

Can we move in our shape?

Can we make a spiral? How?

all together

Let's investigate

"How many rhymes or songs do we know that use our hands?"

Involve the children and parents in this investigation for a week.

How can we record everyone's ideas? Make a tape? Make a book?

"What are all the ways we use our hands in one day?"

How many different ways can we think of?

How can we remember all the different ways? Draw pictures?

"Who do you think has the smallest hands in your home?"

Ask the children to draw around their hands, cut out the shapes and take these home.

Make hand cut-outs of members of your family and friends. What do you find out?

Who has the smallest hands? Who has the biggest?

Bring all your hand cut-outs back to show us, and tell us about the people they belong to. How can we remember which cut-outs belong to which person?

- a large piece of plain material
- paints

above

below

top

bottom

side

beside

next to

between

left

right

Maths learning

Say and use the number names in order in familiar contexts

Use developing mathematical ideas and methods to solve practical problems

Use everyday words to describe position, direction and movement

Hand prints

Spread a large piece of material over a table (part of an old sheet works well). Children paint both hands and print them in a space on the sheet. Write each child's name by her prints. When the sheet is complete you can display the hand prints.

Things to ask

- Whose hands are next to Ben's? Above Kate's?
- Whose hands are between Abi's and Ben's?
- How can I find your hands?
- Is that a left hand or a right hand? How can you tell?

Challenges

Each child has a sheet of paper and does prints of her left and right hands, then numbers the fingers from 1 to 10.

The children make hand prints and cut them out. Stick these side by side on a strip of paper. Use the strip to count in fives and tens, or to measure.

Can the child...

Use words such as 'next to' or 'on top of' to describe the position for her handprint?

Find a clear space for her print so that it does not overlap with another print?

Recognise left hand prints and right hand prints?

Explain her ideas to a group?

Gloves

Muddle the gloves up on the table and ask the children to put them back into pairs.

You will need

● a collection of pairs of gloves or mittens in a variety of colours, patterns and sizes (you could ask the children to bring in old pairs)

one, two...

how many?

count

double

pattern

match

pair

look at

find

Things to ask

● How can you tell if the gloves match?

● How many gloves have you got? How many pairs have you got?

● Hide your glove behind your back. Now describe it to the others. Can they find its partner?

● How many pairs could you make if we had six gloves?

Challenges

The children each put on one glove. Each child has to find the partner who has the matching glove.

Peg pairs of gloves on a washing line. Count them together in twos.

Can the child...

Engage with number problems?

Count how many pairs of gloves he has found?

Match some pairs by recognising similarities?

Work cooperatively as part of a group?

Maths learning

Say and use the number names in order in familiar contexts

Talk about, recognise and recreate simple patterns

Use developing mathematical ideas and methods to solve practical problems

one, two...

how many?

count

guess

altogether

long

short

thick

thin

describe

Maths learning

Say and use the number names in order in familiar contexts

Find one more or one less than a number from 1 to 10

Use language to describe the shape and size of solids and flat shapes

Feelies

Hide a few objects of the same type in a 'feely bag' (for example, plastic dinosaurs inside a furry pencil case). Invite the children to hold and feel the bag. They can try to find out how many objects are inside, and guess what these might be.

Things to ask

- How did you know there were three objects inside?
- How many things would you have if I gave you one more?
- Swap with Courtney. Does she have the same number of things in her bag?
- Can you describe what they feel like?

Challenges

Prepare a 'feely box' (a closed box with a hand hole) containing several different types of object. A child puts her hand inside and counts each type of object by touch.

Children make their own feely bags or boxes, and invent their own questions.

Can the child...

Talk about shapes or objects she touches inside the bag?

Begin to count an irregular arrangement of objects?

Compare two groups of objects and say when they are the same?

Engage with the activity and willingly seek answers?

On your hand

Provide a box of small items, such as buttons. Ask the children to hold out a hand, palm up, and rest it on the table. Invite them to find out how many buttons will fit flat on this hand. They may need to work as partners.

Encourage the children to investigate with lots of different items.

Things to ask

- Can you guess how many things are on your hand before you count?
- How many buttons do you think will fit? More than five? Fewer than five?
- Can you fit more cotton wool balls or more pennies?
- Can you tell us what you have found out?

Challenges

A child must find an item exactly ten of which he can fit on his hand.

The children think of ways to record their counting.

Can the child...

Count irregular arrangements of objects?

Use words such as 'more' and 'fewer'?

Join the discussion by offering comments or asking questions?

Work confidently with a partner?

You will need

- small items such as buttons, pennies, cotton wool balls, paper clips, linking cubes...

one, two...

how many?

count

guess

the same number as

more than

fewer than

next to

Maths learning

Count reliably up to ten everyday objects

Begin to use the vocabulary involved in adding and subtracting

Use developing mathematical ideas and methods to solve practical problems

one, two...

how many?

guess

the same number as

more than

most

fewer than

fewest

least

find

Hide it

ask several children to walk around the room and independently find some small objects to hide in one hand. They bring these back and ask the others to guess how many objects they are holding.

Things to ask

- Is it more than two?
- What's a useful question to ask, to find out how many objects?
- Who is holding the most?
- Who is holding more than Lyndsay?

Challenges

The children put themselves in order according to how many objects each has in her hand.

Each child positions herself on a giant floor number line, according to the number of objects she has in her hand.

Can the child...

Count an irregular arrangement of objects?

Say whether another child has 'more' or 'fewer' objects?

Offer solutions to the problems?

Look for appropriate objects with independence and purpose?

Clap hands

Hold up a wooden numeral or number card and ask the children to clap that many times.

Invite a child to hold up some fingers, or write a number in the air, and ask the others to clap the right number of times.

number

zero

one, two...

how many?

count

one more

one less

listen

Things to ask

● Can you count the claps with me?

● What is 3 and one more? Show me 3 with your fingers… And one more?

● What is one less than 5? Show me 5 with your fingers… And one less?

● Listen to the claps. Can you write that number in the air?

Challenges

Clap your hands while the children listen. Then the children hold up a number card to match your claps.

The children clap one time more than the number says, or one time less.

Can the child...

Recognise and name some numbers?

Match the counting of his claps with the numeral?

Give one more and one less than a given number?

Follow changes in the instructions?

Maths learning
Count reliably up to ten everyday objects
Recognise numerals 1 to 9
Find one more or one less than a number from 1 to 10

A handful

Tell the children to take a handful of pasta shapes and pour them carefully onto a plate or piece of paper. Encourage them to place the pasta shapes in a mound, and also to spread them out flat.

Then show the children a large spoon and discuss whether the pasta shapes will fit onto the spoon. Ask them to investigate and find out what happens.

more

fewer

more than

fewer than

how much?

how many?

compare

too much

too many

work out

Things to ask

● How much space did the pasta shapes take up on the plate?

● Do you think your handful of pasta will fit onto the spoon?

● What will happen if there are too many pasta shapes?

● Can you explain to everyone what you were doing?

Challenges

A child chooses sand, pasta or counters to see how many handfuls fit in a small cup.

The children experiment with different sized spoons and decide which will hold a handful of rice.

Maths learning

Count reliably up to ten everyday objects

Use developing mathematical ideas and methods to solve practical problems

Use language to compare two quantities

Can the child...

Use words such as 'more', 'fewer' and 'too much'?

Discuss how she might solve the problem?

Explain the results of her investigation?

Work independently at the activity?

Touchy

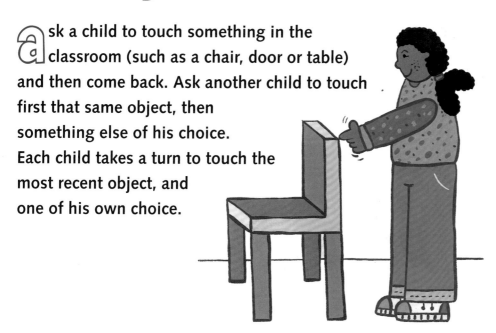

(a)sk a child to touch something in the classroom (such as a chair, door or table) and then come back. Ask another child to touch first that same object, then something else of his choice. Each child takes a turn to touch the most recent object, and one of his own choice.

Things to ask

● How can we help each other to remember the things we touched?

● What's the first thing you will touch? What's the second?

● Can you find something to touch that no one else has thought of?

● At the end of the game, how can we find out how many things were touched altogether?

Challenges

Ask the children to touch the previous two objects as well as their own.

The children touch all previous objects in order, then an object of their own choice.

Can the child...

Remember the order of the objects touched?

Keep track of the last two items touched?

Count accurately the number of things each person touched?

Watch, follow and participate in the game?

You will need

● a variety of ordinary classroom objects

one, two...

order

last

last but one

think

remember

start at

look at

what comes next?

choose

Maths learning

Count reliably up to ten everyday objects

Talk about, recognise and recreate simple patterns

Use developing mathematical ideas and methods to solve practical problems

Finger prints

ask each child to choose a strip of paper and make finger prints along it. Decide together that the finger prints should not overlap, as they would be difficult to count. Encourage each child to guess the number of prints she has made, before counting.

Each strip could then be displayed with the number hidden under a flap; children can guess the number of prints on a strip, count, and check under the flap.

number

one, two...

how many?

guess

the same number as

more than

fewer than

compare

sort

Things to ask

- What paper length will you choose?
- How many finger prints do you think you will fit in on your paper?
- Do you think Karim has done more than five or fewer than five finger prints?
- Which strip of paper do you think has the most prints on?

Challenges

The children sort the finished strips into three collections: more than five finger prints, fewer than five finger prints, and exactly five finger prints.

The children make a finger print strip for every number up to 10, with the number written under a flap.

Can the child...

Make a sensible estimate of the number of finger prints?

Count the finger prints reliably?

Say whether a certain number is more or less than another number?

Select and use resources independently?

Measuring with hands

Groups of children draw around their hands and cut out these outlines. Each group then pools its cut-outs and uses them to find out how many fit side by side along a table top, a book or the carpet.

You will need

- felt-tipped pens
- paper
- scissors
- large objects to measure

Things to ask

- What have you decided to measure?

- Guess first before you try it. How many hands do you think will fit?

- How many hands long is the table top? How many hands wide is it?

- Do you think that you would need more hands to fit along the side of the carpet or along the table top?

Challenges

Each child decides how to record his measurements.

The children measure using just two cut-outs, placing them alternately.

Can the child...

Count the hands by touching one by one?

Make sensible estimates of the length or width of an object?

Use words such as 'longer than' or 'shorter than' when comparing two objects?

Work cooperatively as part of a group?

one, two...

guess

measure

length

width

longer than

shorter than

wider than

edge

next to

Maths learning

Count reliably up to ten everyday objects

Use language to compare two quantities

Use language to describe the size of solids and flat shapes

zero

one, two...

how many?

count

one more

one less

altogether

how many left?

listen

Finger counting

sk the children to hold up one, two, three, four or five fingers. Then invite them to show you one finger more or one finger less.

Now ask them to listen while you slowly drop some pennies into a tin. The children hold up the matching number of fingers. Discuss how many pennies the children heard, then tell them you are going to drop a different number, and ask them to listen again.

Things to ask

● How many fingers have you got on that hand?

● Can you count the fingers with me, touching each one as you say the number? One, two, three, four, five.

● How many penny sounds did you hear?

● Hold up two fingers. If you held up another three, how many would you have?

Challenges

Ask, "If I dropped in one more penny, how many would that be altogether?"

The children use two hands to hold up five fingers.

Can the child...

Show the number of fingers that matches the pennies?

Count the number of fingers reliably up to 5? Up to 10?

Predict the result of adding or taking away pennies or fingers?

Talk about and initiate ideas in the group?

Maths learning

Count reliably up to ten everyday objects

Begin to use the vocabulary involved in adding and subtracting

Find one more or one less than a number from 1 to 10

Hide and seek

@sk the children to work in pairs. Put five counters on the table and ask one child to close her eyes. The other hides some of the counters in his hand, leaving the rest on the table. The first child opens her eyes and has to work out how many counters are hidden in her partner's hand.

Things to ask

● How many counters are there altogether?

● How do you know that Tony is hiding three counters in his hand?

● How do you know that Selma is hiding all of the counters in her hand?

● How did you work out the answer?

Challenges

Give the children more counters.

The children find a way to display what they have worked out.

Can the child...

Recognise that the total number of counters stays the same?

Use his fingers to work out the number of hidden counters?

Predict and explain the number of hidden counters using words such as 'altogether'?

Work cooperatively with a partner?

Hands

You will need

● large counters

one, two...

count on from

how many more?

add

make

sum

total

altogether

take away

leaves

Maths learning

Begin to relate addition to combining two groups of objects

Begin to relate subtraction to 'taking away'

Use language to compare two quantities

Planning and assessment

The mathematics covered in Hands

Significant steps leading to the Early Learning Goals	Hide and seek	Finger counting	Measuring with hands	Finger prints	Touchy	A handful	Clap hands	Hide it	On your hand	Feelies	Gloves	Hand prints
Numbers (as labels and for counting)												
use some number names and number language	★	★	★	★	★	★	★	★	★	★	★	
count with some numbers in the correct order	★	★	★	★	★	★		★	★	★	★	
recognise groups with one, two or three objects	★		★	★						★	★	
count up to four objects by saying one number name for each		★	★	★	★		★		★	★	★	
represent numbers using fingers, pictures or marks on paper				★			★					
recognise numerals up to 9												
count out up to six objects from a larger group	★	★	★	★	★		★		★		★	
count up to or beyond ten objects												
Numbers (for calculating)												
compare two groups of objects and say when the groups are equal in number			★	★				★	★	★		
find the total number of items in two groups by counting all of them	★	★					★					
predict how many objects will be left when one or two are taken away	★	★					★					
say the number that is one more than a given number												
Shape and space												
use positional language to describe location and movement												★
select and use shapes appropriately for a given task									★			
choose to match similar shapes												
describe a simple journey												★
select an example of a named shape												
show awareness of symmetry												
find 2D and 3D shapes that will fit together												
Measures												
use measuring language such as 'high', 'short', 'heavy' and words to describe time			★			★						
talk about instruments we can use for measuring, such as hands and scales			★			★						
order two or three items by length, height, weight or capacity			★									

Containers

In this chapter we use a range of containers to explore capacity, weight, shape and position. We investigate the different ways in which size relates to shape and capacity by asking if one container will fit inside another, or how many spoonfuls of bubbles each container will hold. Similarly, we consider whether 'more objects' always means 'heavier'. We find 2D shapes in 3D objects, and we also practise counting.

Contents

Containers

Let's sing

"Ten shampoo bottles sitting on the wall..."

Collect containers that are all of one type — for example, shampoo bottles. Adapt the song 'Ten Green Bottles' to fit the containers you have collected. Choose the number of containers to start with to suit the children. For example, you might start with 'Five Margarine Tubs' or 'Three Plastic Boxes'.

Can you think of different containers to use in the song?

Let's do

"What is in my bag today?"

Each day hide a different object in a carrier bag.
The children ask you questions to try to guess what is inside the bag. Record how many questions are asked before the correct guess is made. You can also vary the number of objects hidden and ask the children to guess how many there are.

What questions are useful to ask?

Did we need to ask more, or fewer, questions than we asked yesterday?

I've got several objects in my bag. How many do you think there are?

Collection box

Help the children choose what category of objects to collect today: round things, red things, things with numbers on…
Each day ask a different group of children to fill the collection box — and to return the objects to their places at the end of the day.

What is the same about all today's objects?

Would this packet of crayons belong in the collection box today? Why not?

all together

Let's investigate

"What is a container?"

Send several children around the classroom to find a container each. Discuss what we mean by 'a container'. Then make a display of all different kinds of containers. The children can add to the collection from home.

What different things do containers hold?

Are all containers the same shape?

Do all containers have lids? Can you see inside them all?

Why do some containers have writing or numbers on them?

Jelly moulds

Make some jellies, using plastic containers of various shapes as jelly moulds.

What do you notice about the shapes of the jellies? Can you tell which jelly came from which mould?

Do different-shaped jellies taste different?

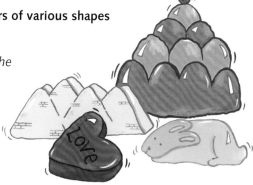

"What goes in here?"

Show the children a selection of different containers (a plastic tub, a straw basket, a cardboard box and so on), and a selection of 'contents' (sand, linking cubes, water and so on). Discuss with the children which containers would be good for holding which contents.

What do we mean by 'good'? How can we check?

larger

smaller

size

full

empty

holds

container

in

inside

Inside, inside, inside

Give each child an object and ask her to put it in a container. Then ask her to put that container inside another container, and that inside another container, and so on.

Things to ask

- Does that fit easily? Is there much room left inside?
- Do you need a bigger or a smaller container than that one?
- How can you tell when one thing fits inside another?
- Can you collect more containers next time?

Challenges

Ask a child to find the smallest container her object will fit into.

Each child makes her own box to hold an object she has chosen.

Can the child...

Use positional words such as 'in' and 'inside'?

Select containers of appropriate size to carry out the task?

Verbalise what she notices about the size and shape of the containers?

Work independently during the activity?

Fill it up

Put a bowl of sand in the middle of the table and give each player a container and a yoghurt pot. Each child takes a turn to roll the dice, say the dice-number and fill his container with that many pots of sand. The game finishes when someone has filled his container.

You will need

- a large bowl of sand
- containers
- small yoghurt pots
- a dice marked '1, 1, 2, 2, 3, 3'

Things to ask

- How many yoghurt pots do you think it will take to fill up your container?

- Is your container nearly full?

- Do you think it will hold another potful?

- How can you keep count of the number of pots you have used?

Challenges

Give the children smaller pots to measure out the sand, so they need more potfuls to fill the containers.

Ask the children to record the number of potfuls they have put in each container by making tallies with beads.

how many?

more than

most

less than

least

count

guess

nearly

compare

full

empty

check

Can the child...

Use language such as 'full' and 'empty'?

Say one number for each potful he adds?

Recognise numerals 1 to 3?

Work as part of a group and take turns?

Maths learning

Say and use the number names in order in familiar contexts

Recognise numerals 1 to 9

Use language to compare two quantities

- very soapy washing up liquid or whisked bubble mix
- a collection of different containers
- a variety of spoons

number

one, two...

how many?

count

guess

more than

less than

size

full

half full

empty

Maths learning

Say and use the number names in order in familiar contexts

Use developing mathematical ideas and methods to solve practical problems

Use language to compare two quantities

Bubble box

Prepare a large bowl of bubbles. Let each child choose a spoon, and invite her to spoon bubbles into the containers. The children can investigate which container holds the most bubbles.

Things to ask

- How will you know when your container is full up?
- Do you think it will take more than five spoonfuls of bubbles to fill your yoghurt pot?
- If you tip the bubbles from your container into Josh's, do you think they'll all fit?
- Can you explain to Carmen what you have been doing?

Challenges

Children spoon all of the bubbles back into the large bowl.

Mix some paint into the mixture and blow bubbles into it with a straw. The children lower paper onto the bubbles to make circular 'bubble prints'.

Can the child...

Use words such as 'full' and 'half full'?

Decide how many bubbles a container might hold?

Say and use some number names appropriately?

Show a high level of involvement in the activity?

Change it

Have a 'change it' session, where children and adults work in small groups to transform a cardboard box into something else. Involve everyone in thinking up ideas — such as boats, space shuttles, buses, beds… Encourage each group to talk about its plans and how it is going to transform its box.

You will need

- large cardboard boxes
- paints
- scissors
- sticky tape or glue
- coloured paper
- some extra adult help

flat

curved

edge

corner

inside

outside

around

in front

behind

left

right

Things to ask

- What gave you the idea to turn this box into a car?
- What shapes have you put on the outside?
- How can you tell the front from the back?
- How can you make sure you can fit inside your box?

Challenges

A child makes a miniature version of his large model using a small box.

The children draw a plan showing the changes they made to the box.

Can the child...

Discuss how he turned the box into something else?

Name or describe shapes he used?

Use language to describe position, direction and movement?

Work cooperatively in a group situation?

Maths learning

Use developing mathematical ideas and methods to solve practical problems

Use language to describe the shape and size of solids and flat shapes

Use everyday words to describe position, direction and movement

31

- plastic flower pots
- sticky labels
- a marker pen
- small plastic bears

number

one, two...

zero

none

how many?

count

the same number as

match

check

Flower pots

Put a sticky label on each pot and number the pots 0 to 5 or 0 to 10. Children work in pairs and together choose a pot. They both read the label. Then the first child puts the right number of teddies inside and the second child picks up this many teddies in her hands. The children then tip out the pot's contents and check if they both have the same number of teddies.

Things to ask

- What do you think that number is?
- How can you check that you both have the same number of teddies?
- Sheila has six teddies and Jenny has five. Who is right? How can you make it right?
- How did you know to leave that pot [showing 0] empty?

Challenges

A child makes her own teddy number track.

Each pair finds how many teddies they have altogether.

Can the child...

Count to check she has the right number of teddies?

Match a collection of teddies to the right numeral?

Recognise and name the numerals?

Work cooperatively with a partner?

Maths learning

Say and use the number names in order in familiar contexts

Count reliably up to ten everyday objects

Recognise numerals 1 to 9

Box wrap

ⓐsk the children to choose a box and some wrapping paper to 'wallpaper' the outside of the box. After discussion you could encourage the children to draw round the box and cut out the shape of each face of the box from their wrapping paper before gluing it on. The children can choose to put objects in their box.

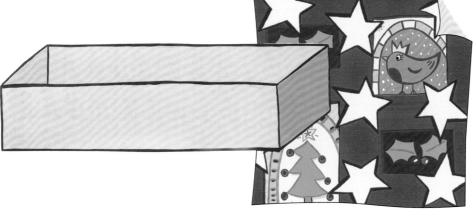

Things to ask

● Which paper will you choose to cover your box? What pattern does it have on it?

● How can you find out how many faces your box has got?

● Can you explain to everyone how you knew what size to cut?

● How many objects have you put in your box?

Challenges

The children find some objects to fit in the wallpapered box.

Challenge the children to turn a box inside out, by cutting one edge.

Can the child...

Use language to describe shape and size?

Talk about his ideas and the decisions he has made?

Use number names when counting objects?

Confidently try a new activity?

You will need

● cardboard boxes
● wrapping paper
● glue or sticky tape
● objects such as building bricks, farm animals or plastic dinosaurs

one, two...

how many?

count

size

bigger

smaller

shape

corner

edge

face

side

Maths learning

Count reliably up to ten everyday objects

Use developing mathematical ideas and methods to solve practical problems

Use language to describe the shape and size of solids and flat shapes

33

You will need

- a water tray
- plastic containers
- small items such as beads, pebbles, conkers, cotton reels...

one, two...

how many?

count

one more

holds

heavier

heaviest

lighter

before

after

Sink the boat

Use a container as a 'boat' and ask a pair of children to find out how many beads the boat will hold before it sinks. They should then try pebbles, cubes or other objects. After a while spent exploring, ask the children to find some way to record their findings as they go along.

Things to ask

- How many pebbles could your boat hold?
- Twelve beads made it sink; so how many could it hold and still stay afloat?
- How might you record what you found out?
- Why did Hamish's boat hold seven cubes before sinking, but only two stones?

Challenges

Ask the children to investigate using a range of containers.

Children make a boat out of modelling dough to hold a play person.

Can the child...

Count the objects accurately?

Work out one more or one less than a number?

Find a way to record what happened?

Talk about her findings, using her own recording to help remember?

Container counts

Show the children a collection of containers, such as a very large packing box, a cereal box and a film canister. Discuss how many things you might be able to put in each container. Try counting how many children can stand in the packing box, and how many buttons will go in a film canister. Then ask each pair of children to choose a container and fill it with objects. The children find out which type of object they can fit most of in the container.

Things to ask

● What have you chosen to put in your container?

● How many plastic dinosaurs do you think will fit in the round tub?

● What do you think is the best way to count how many things are in the box?

● How will you remember the number of cotton reels in your tin?

one, two...

how many?

count

more

fewer

size

smaller

smallest

bigger

biggest

the same as

Challenges

Challenge the children to find a box which holds eight dice.

The children find out how many containers fit into a plastic crate or a shopping bag.

Can the child...

Select appropriate objects with which to fill his container?

Count an irregular collection of objects?

Compare two groups of objects and say which is more?

Work cooperatively with a partner?

Maths learning

Count reliably up to ten everyday objects

Use developing mathematical ideas and methods to solve practical problems

Use language to compare two quantities

You will need

- small boxes
- a collection of small objects
- an ordinary 1–6 dice

one, two...

zero

how many?

count

too many

too few

enough

one more

one less

same as

check

Maths learning

Count reliably up to ten everyday objects

Use language to compare two numbers

Use developing mathematical ideas and methods to solve practical problems

The 'same as' game

Give each child a box and ask him to begin by putting three things in it. Each child then takes a turn to roll the dice. The aim is to make the number of objects in his box match the dice number. When a child needs more objects, he should take them from the other children's boxes. When he has too many objects, he should hand them out to other players. In either case, he may choose which child or children he wishes to give to or take from.

Things to ask

- How many things have you got in your box?
- Will you need to put things in, or take things out, of your box?
- What would happen if you threw a 6?
- How did you work out how many things to take out?

Challenges

The children start with a larger number of objects.

A child throws two dice: one to find how many objects to take out of her box; one to find how many to put in.

Can the child...

Recognise the dice dot patterns?

Use words such as 'more' and 'less' when playing the game?

Work out how many more or fewer objects she needs in her box?

Play the game cooperatively, taking turns as part of a group?

Pirate's treasure

Hide some treasure in the sand and give each child a collecting bag. The children take it in turns to roll the dice. Every time a child rolls a skull and crossbones, he can search for a piece of treasure to put in his bag. When all the treasure has been found, the bags are weighed to see who has collected the most treasure.

Things to ask

● What treasure did you find?

● How will you find out whose treasure weighs the most?

● Reema's bag was very light. Why was that? What sorts of treasure did she find?

● Biniam's bag feels the heaviest but he only has three things. Why is that?

Challenges

The children play in larger groups, so the task of finding whose bag is heaviest is more complex.

The children record what treasure they found.

Can the child...

Use words such as 'heavier' and 'lighter'?

Describe the found items using the language of shape?

Show some understanding of how balances are used?

Play the game cooperatively with a partner?

You will need

● a dice with skull and crossbones on three sides, and three blank sides

● 'treasure' such as necklaces, rings and medals

● a container of sand

● bags

● bucket scales

one, two...

weigh

lighter

lightest

heavier

heaviest

balance

scales

Maths learning

Use developing mathematical ideas and methods to solve practical problems

Use language to compare two quantities

Use language to describe the shape and size of solids

Containers

One to one

You will need

- egg boxes or bun tins
- conkers, buttons, cotton reels...
- wooden numerals or number cards

how many?

count

the same number as

match

full

repeat

more

most

fewer

fewest

least

Give each child or pair of children an egg box or bun tin, and ask them to put one object in each compartment. When the tray is full, ask the children to find the matching wooden numeral or number card to put next to the tray. Give each child the opportunity to fill several different types of tray.

Things to ask

- How will you know when the tray is full?
- How many conkers do you think you will need for this tray? How can you find out?
- Are there two trays which hold the same number of things?
- Which tray contains the most/fewest things? Can you tell by reading the number?

Challenges

Children put two objects in each compartment, count the objects in twos and find the number card to match.

The children compare an empty egg box with an empty bun tray and decide which will hold more objects.

Maths learning

Count reliably up to ten everyday objects

Recognise numerals 1 to 9

Use language to compare two numbers

Can the child...

Keep track of where she started counting?

Choose the correct number label for each tray?

Explain the connection between the number of objects the tray holds and the number label?

Work systematically to complete the task?

Lids on!

Put out a collection of containers with the lids off, and give each child three of the lids. The children take turns to choose one container and try each of their lids on it. If a lid fits, the child can keep the container; if not, he must wait for his next turn. The game ends when all the lids are on their containers.

bigger

smaller

size

match

guess

wide

wider

narrow

narrower

shape

circle

square

Things to ask

● Can you explain what you have to do in this game?

● How did you know your lid would fit that container?

● What shape would this container's lid be?

● How could you record which lid fits on which container?

Challenges

Share out the containers first and ask the children to find lids to fit.

Make imprints with the lids in damp sand; the children decide which lid fits which print.

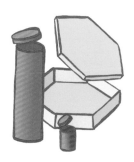

Can the child...

Explain the best way to match the lids and containers?

Use the language of shape to describe lids or containers?

Use the language of measurement to describe the size of the lids or containers?

Make decisions independently during the game?

Maths learning

Use developing mathematical ideas and methods to solve practical problems

Use language to compare two quantities

Use language to describe the shape and size of solids and flat shapes

planning and assessment

The mathematics covered in Containers

Significant steps leading to the Early Learning Goals	Lids on!	One to one	Pirate's treasure	The 'same as' game	Container counts	Sink the boat	Box wrap	Flower pots	Change it	Bubble box	Fill it up	Inside, inside, inside
Numbers (as labels and for counting)												
use some number names and number language		★	★	★	★	★	★	★		★	★	
count with some numbers in the correct order		★	★	★	★	★	★	★		★	★	
recognise groups with one, two or three objects		★		★		★	★	★				
count up to four objects by saying one number name for each		★	★	★		★	★	★		★	★	
represent numbers using fingers, pictures or marks on paper		★			★	★					★	
recognise numerals up to 9				★	★	★		★			★	
count out up to six objects from a larger group			★	★	★			★		★	★	
count up to or beyond ten objects												
Numbers (for calculating)												
compare two groups of objects and say when the groups are equal in number		★		★	★			★				
find the total number of items in two groups by counting all of them							★		★			
predict how many objects will be left when one or two are taken away							★	★	★			
say the number that is one more than a given number							★	★				
Shape and space												
use positional language to describe location and movement	★											★
select and use shapes appropriately for a given task	★											★
choose to match similar shapes												★
describe a simple journey									★			
select an example of a named shape	★						★		★			★
show awareness of symmetry	★											
find 2D and 3D shapes that will fit together	★											
Measures												
use measuring language such as 'high', 'short', 'heavy' and words to describe time	★		★		★	★	★		★	★	★	★
talk about instruments we can use for measuring, such as hands and scales			★		★		★		★	★	★	
order two or three items by length, height, weight or capacity	★		★									★

Teddy bears

In this chapter we count and describe teddy bears and sort them by similarities and differences. We talk about their size, and arrange them in various ways, such as in order of height or in different patterns.

We try out some sophisticated adding and subtracting to make sure the bears all have the right number of chips to eat, and that they get off the bus at the right stop. We can even go on 'bear hunts' to practise our position and direction words.

Contents

Teddy bears

Let's sing

"Teddy bear, teddy bear"

Sing the action rhyme:

"Teddy bear, teddy bear, turn around,

Teddy bear, teddy bear, touch the ground…"

Then ask the children to make up their own versions.

What other ways can Teddy move? Can you show us?

Can you draw one of Teddy's actions?
Let's make a book of all your pictures.

Let's do

"This bear likes…"

Sit in a circle and pass round a teddy bear. As each child holds the bear she thinks of something the bear likes and says it aloud: "This bear likes ice cream"; "This bear likes skipping"; "This bear likes singing." To make the game harder, ask each child to repeat the previous player's idea before adding her own.

What can we do to help us remember what the bear likes?

The three bears' house

The three bears had three bowls, three spoons, three chairs and three beds.

What other things did they need three of? Did they need three TVs? Three toothbrushes? Three ovens?

What did they need six of? Socks? Gloves?

all together

Let's investigate

Shaggy bear stories

Collect stories about bears from different sources.

How many stories can we find?

How can we let other people know what we are doing, so that they can join in and help?

How shall we organise our stories?

Where shall we keep our collection?

Bring a teddy bear from home

Record and display the number of bears in the collection, as more are added each day. Ask the children to draw pictures of the teddy bears, and use these to make a counting diary of each day's collection.

How many bears are here today?

Can you count them?

How many more do we need to draw today?

Old and new

Ask the class to find out which bear is the oldest in the class collection, and which is the newest.

How can we find out?

How old is the oldest bear?

Who is the oldest person in your family? And the newest?

measure

size

enough

not enough

too much

long

longer

short

shorter

tall

wide

narrow

Put the bear to bed

Invite a group of children to make a bed for the teddy bear, with a pillow and a cover. The group may need an adult to help. Display the bed with its sleeping bear for everyone to look at and discuss.

Things to ask

- How can you make sure that the bear will fit in his bed?
- Why did you choose that size pillow?
- How did you know that this cover would be big enough to keep your bear warm?
- Susie says that cover is too small. How can you make a cover the right size?

Challenge

The group or individual children can make other things for the bear's bedroom.

Children make a bed for a giant bear.

Can the child...

Measure or use direct comparison to estimate if the bear will fit?

Use words such as 'shorter' and 'longer'?

Select a suitably shaped box?

Discuss what she has done?

All sorts

ask the children to sort out the bears, according to different criteria. For instance, explain that only bears with outdoor clothing can play outside, or only small bears can ride in the cart. Invite the children to think of and draw a label for each set.

Teddy bears

You will need
- a large collection of different teddy bears
- drawing paper or card
- felt-tipped pens
- luggage labels

Things to ask

- Are all these bears similar in some way?
- What is the same about this group of bears?
- Why does this bear not go in this set?
- What does your label tell us about these bears?

Challenges

Hide the label for a set. The children decide what the bears have in common and draw a new label for the set.

Children make another set using different objects.

Can the child...

Sort the bears according to the criteria suggested?

Say why a particular bear does or does not belong to a particular group?

Think of and draw a label to describe a set?

Initiate ideas and talk about what he is doing?

sort

group

set

compare

size

long

short

tall

pick out

wide

Maths learning

Use developing mathematical ideas and methods to solve practical problems

Use language to compare two quantities

Use language to describe the shape and size of solids and flat shapes

You will need

● teddy bears
● three different-
coloured teddy
bears' outfits (red
hat, top and
trousers; blue hat,
top and trousers;
yellow hat, top
and trousers)
● bear outlines
drawn on paper

one, two...

sort

match

compare

arrange

change

colour

work out

check

What will bear wear?

(a)sk a pair of children to think up and try out lots of different combinations of outfits for their teddy bears to wear. They may want a simple outline of the bear on paper, on which to record the different outfits.

Things to ask

● How will we know if you have already tried a particular outfit?

● How can you show all the combinations you have thought of?

● Is there a way of doing this which helps you get all the different mixtures?

● How many different outfits are possible with these clothes? How do you know?

Challenges

A child tries to make two different bear oufits.

The children make a record of all the different combinations they find.

Maths learning
Count reliably up to ten
everyday objects
Talk about, recognise and
recreate simple patterns
Use developing
mathematical ideas and
methods to solve practical
problems

Can the child...

Think of different combinations?

Recognise when one combination is the same as another?

Make a record of her work?

Work cooperatively with a partner?

Lead the way

sk one child to close his eyes. Give another child a teddy bear and a set of arrows. The second child hides the bear and lays a path with the arrows. The first child then opens his eyes and follows the arrow path to find the bear.

As the searcher moves along, help the rest of the class to describe where he is going: "Under the table, around the chair…" and give a clap when he reaches the bear.

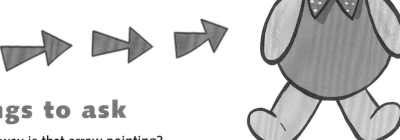

You will need

- teddy bear
- arrows made from card or paper

over

under

around

left

right

forward

backward

across

along

through

towards

away from

Things to ask

- Which way is that arrow pointing?
- Was it easy to find the bear? How did the arrows help you?
- How can Sian make it take longer to find the bear?
- Can you describe Fiona's path back to us with the bear?

Challenges

A child looks at the arrows and describes the path to the searcher before he embarks on his quest.

The children draw the route to the bear on paper.

Can the child…

Understand and explain the purpose of the arrows?

Describe the direction in which the arrows lead?

Describe how someone would get back along the arrow path?

Explore and take an active part in the game?

Maths learning

Talk about, recognise and recreate simple patterns

Use developing mathematical ideas and methods to solve practical problems

Use everyday words to describe position, direction and movement

under

top

on

in

inside

in front of

behind

beside

next to

opposite

between

Bear hunt

S et up a bear hunt in the playground by putting teddy bears in lots of different places — under the bench, on top of the climbing frame, next to the gate... Send the children off in pairs to find a bear and bring it back, telling you where they found it.

Things to ask

● Where did you find your bear?

● Can you remember where Hakan and Isobel found a bear?

● Who found a bear under something? So how many bears were under something?

● How many bears did we find all together?

Challenges

Ask the children to draw where they found their bears.

Pairs of children play 'hunt the bear': one child hides the bear, then helps her partner find it by using words such as 'near' and 'far'.

Can the child...

Use number names in order?

Describe where the bear was found, using words such as 'next to' and 'under'?

Help to count the total number of found bears?

Work cooperatively with a partner?

In the bears' house

Put up a 'number of the day' in the home corner. This number says how many bears can come to tea, and how many things each bear can have to eat. Ask the children to help each other set the table for the bears.

Teddy bears

You will need

- teddy bears
- large number cards
- home corner equipment: table and tea things

number

one, two...

how many?

count

total

altogether

share out

enough

not enough

check

Things to say

- How many bears are coming today?
- How many cups will you need?
- How can you check that each bear has the same number of chips?
- Did you have enough cakes for each bear to have four?

Challenges

Children make invitations asking more bears to come to tea.

Children decide how much food they will need for a teddy bears' picnic.

Can the child...

Read and say the number of the day?

Count this number of objects and check the count?

Find out if there are enough biscuits to give the bears the right number?

Work cooperatively in a group?

Maths learning

Count reliably up to ten everyday objects

Recognise numerals 1 to 9

Begin to use the vocabulary involved in adding and subtracting

you will need

● six plastic cups
● at least twelve
  small plastic bears
● twenty red bears

zero

one, two...

how many?

count

the same
number as

more

fewer

match

remember

Doubles

Hide little groups of one, two, and three bears under plastic cups. The children take turns to pick up two cups. If a child finds the same number of bears under both cups, she wins a red bear. If the numbers are different, she replaces the two cups.

Things to ask

● Which cups will you look under?

● How many bears were there under the first cup you chose?

● How did you know there were the same number of bears under both cups?

● How many bears did you have altogether?

Challenges

Increase the number of bears under the cups.

The child wins a red bear if the bears under her cups add up to 5.

Can the child...

Use number names when explaining what happened?

Recognise small numbers of objects without counting?

Use language such as 'more' or 'less'?

Play this new game confidently?

All in order

Put a collection of bears out on the table. Children work together to find which is the tallest bear and which is the shortest.

Things to ask

● How will you find which bear is tallest?

● You know that Red Ted is taller than Fuzzy Ted. What will you do next?

● Which bear is just a bit taller than this bear? Which bear is a lot taller than this bear?

● Which bear is the tallest? Which is the shortest?

Challenge

Children make a height chart for the bears.

The children rearrange the bears in order of width (or 'fatness').

Can the child...

Compare the lengths of two bears directly?

Use a ribbon, measuring tape or stick to compare the bears?

Find a way to compare the lengths of more than two bears?

Show a high level of involvement in the group?

order

measure

compare

short

shorter

shortest

tall

taller

tallest

start from

Maths learning

Use developing mathematical ideas and methods to solve practical problems

Use language to compare two quantities

Use language to describe the shape and size of solids and flat shapes

51

Teddy
bears

you will need

● several different
teddy bears, all
dressed up
● an empty
cardboard box

one, two...

match

tall

short

top

on

inside

front

back

left

right

My bear

Hold up an empty cardboard box and describe a bear from the collection that you want for your box. For example, "The bear I want in the box has a hat with dots and four buttons on her jacket." Invite a child to find the correct bear and put it in the box.

Play the game several times, then offer the box to the children. Each child takes a turn to ask for a bear.

Things to ask

● What can we say about this bear?
● How would you describe the smallest bear?
● How can we check whether Maeve has the right bear?
● This bear has trousers on, but how do you know it's not the bear Sammi wanted?

Challenges

Change the collection. The more 'similar' the bears in the collection are, the more challenging this activity will be.

Use negatives to describe the bears, such as, "I want the bear without a hat, and who is not blue."

Can the child...

Listen and respond to a description?

Find the bear that was described?

Use shape words to describe a bear?

Take on the role of Describer?

Maths learning

Use developing
mathematical ideas and
methods to solve practical
problems

Use language to describe
the shape and size of
solids

Use everyday words to
describe position

Compare the bear

Begin by asking each child to choose a bear. Then ask each child to find a ribbon that is longer than his bear, one that is shorter than his bear and one that is about the same length.

measure

compare

guess

about the same as

just over

just under

length

longer than

shorter than

start from

Things to ask

● Which ribbon do you think is the same length as your bear?

● Where should you put your ribbon to compare it with the bear?

● How did you find out that this piece of ribbon is longer than your bear?

● Can you guess which ribbon might be about the same length as your bear before you measure it?

Challenges

Ask the children to draw what they have found out.

A child must find something else the same length as his bear.

Can the child...

Use words such as 'longer than' and 'shorter than'?

Choose a ribbon the same length as the bear?

Compare the lengths of the ribbons and the bear?

Persist with more complex extended tasks?

Maths learning

Use developing mathematical ideas and methods to solve practical problems

Use language to compare two quantities

Use everyday words to describe position, direction and movement

Bears in a bus queue

ask each child to choose ten bears and line them up in a bus queue. The children take turns to push along the 'bus', spin the spinner and put that many bears on board. The activity continues until all the bears are on the bus.

Things to ask

● How many bears have you got in your bus queue?

● How do you know how many bears to put on the bus?

● What shall we do if you have fewer bears than the number on the spinner?

● What's the most bears you can put on the bus at one time?

Challenges

Start with all the bears on the bus and ask the children to use the spinner to see how many get off.

Give the children two spinners: one to decide how many bears get on; and one to say how many get off the bus.

Can the child...

Say and use the number names on the spinner?

Count out bears from a larger group?

Compare two groups of bears using words such as 'same as' or 'fewer'?

Take turns and work cooperatively to push the bus along?

How many missing?

ask the children to look at all the bears on the table, then cover the bears with a large piece of material. Pull some out and place them on top of the cloth. The children see if they can work out how many bears are still underneath the cloth.

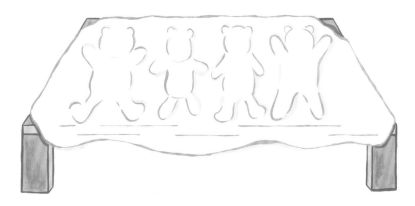

Things to ask

● How many bears were there to start with?

● How many bears did I take out?

● How many bears are left under the cloth?

● How did you work it out?

Challenges

Remove bears secretly, then take off the cloth. The children guess the number of missing bears.

Change the number of bears each time you hide some. Count them first, and continue as before.

Can the child...

Count and remember the number of bears under the cloth?

Make a thoughtful guess at the missing number?

Explain a way to work out the number of missing bears?

Discuss ideas on how to solve the problem?

You will need

● four or five teddy bears

● a large piece of material

one, two...

how many?

add

altogether

take away

leave

how many have gone?

one less, two less...

Maths learning

Count reliably up to ten everyday objects

Begin to use the vocabulary involved in adding and subtracting

Begin to relate subtraction to 'taking away'

The mathematics covered in Teddy bears

Significant steps leading to the Early Learning Goals

Learning goal	How many missing?	Bears in a bus queue	Compare the bear	My bear	All in order	Doubles	In the bears' house	Bear hunt	Lead the way	What will bear wear?	All sorts	Put the bear to bed
Numbers (as labels and for counting)												
use some number names and number language	★	★		★		★	★	★		★		
count with some numbers in the correct order	★	★		★			★	★		★		
recognise groups with one, two or three objects	★	★		★		★	★	★				
count up to four objects by saying one number name for each	★	★		★			★	★		★		
represent numbers using fingers, pictures or marks on paper							★					
recognise numerals up to 9												
count out up to six objects from a larger group		★					★	★		★		
count up to or beyond ten objects												
Numbers (for calculating)												
compare two groups of objects and say when the groups are equal in number						★	★					
find the total number of items in two groups by counting all of them		★				★	★					
predict how many objects will be left when one or two are taken away	★	★					★					
say the number that is one more than a given number							★					
Shape and space												
use positional language to describe location and movement				★				★	★		★	★
select and use shapes appropriately for a given task				★				★	★	★	★	★
choose to match similar shapes											★	
describe a simple journey									★			
select an example of a named shape				★								
show awareness of symmetry												
find 2D and 3D shapes that will fit together												
Measures												
use measuring language such as 'high', 'short', 'heavy' and words to describe time			★		★							★
talk about instruments we can use for measuring, such as hands and scales			★		★							★
order two or three items by length, height, weight or capacity			★		★							★

Green peppers

This chapter delights and intrigues us with the unexpected. Patterns 'go wrong', green peppers print red, and 2D shapes appear magically when we print with or cut 3D objects. We count, sort and arrange all manner of green objects: food, and fruit and vegetables. We think about 'green' and 'not green', and get the chance to express our feelings about what we do — and don't — like to eat!

A word of warning: green pepper seeds can be toxic, so de-seed cut peppers very thoroughly.

Contents

Green peppers

Let's sing

"Five green peppers"

Sing this song to the tune of 'Ten Green Bottles'. Act it out using a bowl of peppers and a 'monster' to eat them — or choose a child to pretend to eat them, and help her hide the peppers in her jersey.

"Five green peppers sitting in a bowl,
Five green peppers sitting in a bowl,
And if one green pepper should then be eaten whole,
There'll be four green peppers sitting in a bowl…"

Let's do

"Green pepper, red pepper, green pepper, red pepper…"

Repeat this pattern aloud with the children.

Can you keep it going?

Can you see the pattern in your mind?

What can we do to help us remember it?

How can we change the pattern or add to it?

Pick up a pepper

Pass a green pepper around the class to that everyone can have a close look and a feel.

What words could we use to describe the pepper?

How would you describe its shape?

What does it feel like? Is the skin smooth or rough?

Is it heavy or light?

all together

Let's investigate

Tongue twister

Read aloud to the class:

"Peter Piper picked a peck of pickled pepper
A peck of pickled pepper Peter Piper picked.
If Peter Piper picked a peck of pickled pepper,
Where's the peck of pickled pepper Peter Piper picked?"

Can you guess how many 'p's there are in this tongue-twister?

How can we find out?

"What other green things do we eat?"

Ask the children to name some green foods.

How many can we think of?

How can we collect and record our ideas?

You will need

● green and red
objects such as
cubes, plastic
fruit, small
plastic bears,
beads, bricks…

every other

pattern

same

different

continue

repeat

shape

match

what comes
next?

colour

Make a mistake

Discuss with the children ideas of pattern making. Help them make some repeating colour patterns with cubes. Then tell the children that the next time you repeat the pattern, you are going to make a mistake — and ask if they can spot it.

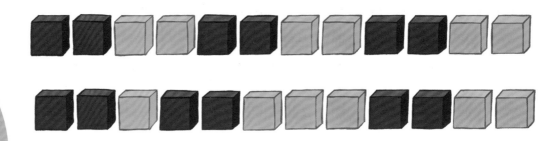

Things to ask

● Green, red, green, red… What comes next?

● Do you think that blue cube should be in our pattern?

● How could you record your pattern so that your friend could make it again tomorrow?

● Yasmin's cube pattern goes 'green, green, red, green, green, red, green, yellow…' Can you see her deliberate mistake?

Challenges

One child starts a pattern and a friend finishes it.

Make a display of patterns: 'Can you spot our deliberate mistakes?'

Can the child...

Continue a pattern that has been started?

Make a two-colour pattern of her own?

Discuss or describe her pattern?

Sustain her interest in the activity for a length of time?

Print a red pepper

Put out some red paint and invite the children to make a print using a green pepper. Ask them to predict what colour the print will be.

Allow the children to experiment with printing in different colours, using various objects on the table. Encourage them to guess what shape each object will make before they try it out.

Things to ask

● What print shape do you think the pepper/cube/carrot will make? Why do you think that?

● Did you guess that shape correctly? Was the shape that the cotton reel made a surprise?

● Do all the peppers print exactly the same shape? Why is that?

● What words can we use to describe shapes?

Challenges

Children try to fit as many different things as they can on the paper.

Children identify which objects were used to make which prints.

Can the child...

Place the objects so that the prints do not overlap?

Make a sensible guess about the shape of the print and talk about the outcome?

Notice and talk about similarities and differences between the prints?

Maintain focus during the activity and try a variety of objects?

You will need

- green and red apples
- a knife
- paper for printing
- coloured paints

whole

half

middle

part

same

different

shape

pattern

round

star

Maths learning

Talk about, recognise and recreate simple patterns

Use language to describe the shape and size of solids and flat shapes

Use everyday words to describe position

Apple stars

Discuss with the children the possibility of finding a star inside an apple. Take a green apple and cut it in half horizontally. Ask the children to look at the cross-section and describe what they see. You can try this again with a red apple.

Things to ask

- Will it look the same if we cut the apple in half a different way?
- When you cut something in half how many pieces do you get?
- We have cut lots of apples in half. If we muddled them up, could you put the halves back together?
- Can you describe the apple half to everybody?

Challenges

The children draw the cross-section, then show and explain their work to one another.

Help the children to print designs on a sheet of paper using the apple halves.

Can the child...

Match the halves that have been cut up?

Talk about the shapes and patterns she can see?

Use words such as 'half' and 'whole'?

Sustain an interest in what happens?

Green things

Give two children one minute to collect green things from around the room in their bucket. Ask the rest of the children to help you time them using a sand timer. The two Collectors then count and record their objects. The other children join in with the counting and ask questions about the collection. This can be played daily until everyone has been a Collector.

Things to ask

● Let's all count Jayshree's green things: one, two…

● Does that book count as green? Put thumbs up if you think it does.

● What is the smallest/heaviest/softest thing you found?

● Do you think you can put all the green things back in the right places in one minute? We'll time you.

Challenges

Set a target for the children to collect more green things than the day before.

Ask the children to collect something different.

Can the child…

Understand when to start, and when to stop, collecting?

Make a good attempt at counting the objects?

Make a decision about what 'green' is, in this context?

Put each object back in the right place?

Green peppers

You will need

● a sand timer
● a bucket
● a variety of large and small classroom objects, of different colours

measure

time

how many?

count

one, two…

more

fewer

not

colour

Maths learning

Say and use the number names in order in familiar contexts

Count reliably up to ten everyday objects

Use developing mathematical ideas and methods to solve practical problems

63

sort

how many?

how many
more?

count

one, two...

check

list

match

the same as

Market stall

With the children, set up a class 'market stall' with boxes of fruit and vegetables. Once the stall has been set up, ask the class to help you count and record how many of each item you have, in order to make a stock list.

Things to ask

- How many green peppers are there? Count with me: one, two…
- How shall we record the bananas we have just counted?
- Alana has only found seven green peppers. How many more does she need to find?
- There are no melons in the box. How many are missing?

Challenges

Children sort the fruit and vegetables to set the stall up.

Incorporate the stock list into the children's play. They can use it to check the goods before opening the stall in the morning and and closing it at home time.

Can the child...

Count how many of each thing she has sorted?

Count how many items she has altogether?

Use the stock list to check the number of items on the stall?

Work with others in a group?

Salad day

Spend some time looking at and discussing the food. Then ask the children to work in small groups helping everyone to prepare the food. Keep each food item separate.

Later, lay out the prepared salad items and give each person a paper plate. Children and adults take turns to go up and choose what they would like to eat.

Things to ask

- What would you like to help prepare?
- Do you think there will be enough food for everyone?
- How many different things did you eat?
- What can we do to help us remember what we had to eat today?

Challenges

A child finds someone who chose the same food as himself.

Ask the children what they ate, and invite them to make a menu of the food.

Can the child...

Sort and count the vegetables?

Remember what he had to eat?

Make and interpret a record of the salad he ate?

Show interest and involvement in getting the food ready?

sort

how many?

count

check

same

different

amount

each

left over

enough

Maths learning

Say and use the number names in order in familiar contexts

Count reliably up to ten everyday objects

Use developing mathematical ideas and methods to solve practical problems

sort

put

not

how many?

count

one, two...

compare

more than

fewer than

Maths learning

Say and use the number names in order in familiar contexts

Count reliably up to ten everyday objects

Use language to compare two quantities

Green... not green

Give each pair of children a tray of fruit and vegetables and ask them to sort out which are green and which are not green. Suggest the children think of a way to record their work.

The children could then repeat the activity, this time sorting into, say, red and not red.

Things to ask

- What do you need to do first?
- How many green fruits and vegetables are there?
- Can you show us a fruit that is not green?
- How can you record that?

Challenges

Children can count and record how many there are of each colour — and each time count and record how many there are in the 'not' set.

Children look for another classroom object that could belong in each set.

Can the child...

Sort the objects according to the rule suggested?

Use counting to find out 'how many'?

Think of a way to record her sorting?

Work systematically to complete the task?

Peas in a pod

sk the children to guess how many peas are inside a pea pod. Invite each child to write down his guess on a Post-It note. Then together open the pods, count the seeds and record the number.

Talk about the various guesses and the actual number of peas, and encourage the children to ask each other questions about their counting.

Things to ask

- How many do you think there might be?
- Let's look at all our guesses. Which is the highest number? Which is the lowest?
- How many peas were there?
- Who guessed a number near the right number? How can we find out?

Challenges

Children work together in pairs independently to count the peas.

Children record the number of peas on a number line.

guess

estimate

how many?

count

one, two...

inside

greatest

most

fewest

least

close to

Can the child...

Guess a sensible number of peas?

Write down the number he has guessed?

Make a comment about this counting based on his observations?

Show an interest in how the seeds are counted?

Maths learning

Say and use the number names in order in familiar contexts

Count reliably up to ten everyday objects

Recognise numerals 1 to 9

- green peppers, washed and cut into small pieces
- paper or card
- a marker pen

how many?

count

zero

one, two...

sort

group

same

different

before

after

Maths learning

Say and use the number names in order in familiar contexts

Use developing mathematical ideas and methods to solve practical problems

Use language to compare quantities

I like green peppers

Tell the children they are going to have a pepper tasting. First, make a chart with the children; ask them to fill in their names according to whether they like green peppers, don't like green peppers, or are not sure.

Let everyone try a piece of pepper. Then go back through the chart with the children and ask if any of them have changed their minds.

🫑	⊗	?
Leon maia	Harry	Namanh Juan

Things to ask

- How many children say they like green peppers? Count the names with me: one, two…
- How many don't like green peppers? How many are not sure?
- Which group has the most names in?
- How many children say they like green peppers now? Is that more or less than before?

Challenges

Children could make a similar 'taste chart' for red and yellow peppers, or other vegetables.

A child makes a list of six children who like both green peppers and red tomatoes.

Can the child...

Write her name in the appropriate space?

Use the completed chart to gain information?

Count and compare the number of names in each category?

Approach this new activity positively?

Five on a plate

Give each child a plate and five green peppers or other vegetables or fruit. Ask the children to put some of their peppers on one side of the plate and the rest on the other side. They should then try another arrangement. Encourage the children to explore all the different combinations; the only rule is that all five peppers must be used each time.

Things to ask

- Iman has two peppers on this side and three peppers on this side. How many is that all together?

- Tom has three peppers here and two there. Is this the same as Iman's plate?

- Chau has put all five peppers on this side. How many are there on the other side?

- Have you tried that arrangement already? How can you be sure?

Challenges

When the children have tried plenty of arrangements, ask them to think of a way to record these.

Children try using more peppers.

Can the child...

Separate the objects in different ways?

Recognise that the total number of objects is still the same?

Think of a way to record what he has done?

Carry out the activity independently?

Green peppers

You will need

- a paper plate with a line drawn down the middle
- real or play fruit or vegetables

how many?

zero

one, two...

arrange

add

make

altogether

total

is the same as

Maths learning

Count reliably up to ten everyday objects

Begin to use the vocabulary involved in adding and subtracting

Begin to relate addition to combining two groups of objects

69

You will need

- four soft toys
- four paper plates
- play food
- a prepared chart indicating which food each toy likes

match

find

not

check

how many?

count

one, two...

zero

Maths learning

Say and use the number names in order in familiar contexts

Count reliably up to ten everyday objects

Use developing mathematical ideas and methods to solve practical problems

Get the dinner ready

Set a pair of children the task of preparing a plate full of food for each toy. They should use the chart to find out which food each toy will want.

Suggest to the children that they check each other's work when they have finished.

Things to ask

- How do you know that Rag Doll likes sandwiches?
- How many of the toys like bananas?
- How many things does Teddy have on his plate?
- Could you make a chart like this showing what you would like to be given for dinner?

Challenges

Children can draw up a similar chart showing what other toys like.

A group of children work together to make a chart showing everybody's favourite foods.

Can the child...

Use the information on the chart to carry out the task?

Help to check someone else's work?

Talk about the activity when it is completed?

Work well in a pair and share fairly?

Ugh — yuck!

Have a discussion about 'things we really don't like to eat,' then ask the children to draw their least favourite food. Gather the children together and ask them, one by one, to stick their pictures up where everyone can see. Arrange the pictures so that each category of 'least favourites' is grouped together.

Things to ask

- Do you think that everyone will draw something different or will some people draw the same thing?

- What is your least favourite food? How will you draw it?

- How many people have drawn mushrooms?

- Stand up and hold hands with the other people who drew what you drew.

Challenges

Arrange the pictures to form a block graph, and count and compare the numbers of each category.

Use the computer to make a block graph using the information you have collected.

Can the child...

Draw a picture of his least favourite food?

Notice that another child's idea is the same as, or different from, his own?

Suggest a way to group pictures of the same food?

Participate in the discussion?

planning and assessment

The mathematics covered in Green peppers

Objective	Make a mistake	Print a red pepper	Apple stars	Green things	Market stall	Salad day	Green… not green	Peas in a pod	I like green peppers	Five on a plate	Get the dinner ready	Ugh — yuck!
Numbers (as labels and for counting)												
use some number names and number language	★			★	★	★	★	★	★	★	★	★
count with some numbers in the correct order	★			★	★	★	★	★	★	★	★	★
recognise groups with one, two or three objects	★			★	★	★	★	★	★	★	★	★
count up to four objects by saying one number name for each				★	★	★	★	★	★		★	★
represent numbers using fingers, pictures or marks on paper												
recognise numerals up to 9												
count out up to six objects from a larger group				★		★	★	★	★	★		
count up to or beyond ten objects												
Numbers (for calculating)												
compare two groups of objects and say when the groups are equal in number	★			★	★				★	★		★
find the total number of items in two groups by counting all of them					★					★		
predict how many objects will be left when one or two are taken away												
say the number that is one more than a given number												
Shape and space												
use positional language to describe location and movement		★	★	★								
select and use shapes appropriately for a given task				★					★			
choose to match similar shapes		★	★									
describe a simple journey												
select an example of a named shape		★										
show awareness of symmetry		★	★									
find 2D and 3D shapes that will fit together			★									
Measures												
use measuring language such as 'high', 'short', 'heavy' and words to describe time						★						
talk about instruments we can use for measuring, such as hands and scales				★								
order two or three items by length, height, weight or capacity												

Squares

This section explores and establishes the idea of what a square is. We look for squares to jump in, fill up or colour, play games on square tracks and handle cubes — and even 'explode' a square! We consider the properties of a square and other shapes, both 2D and 3D, and make them out of different materials.

The activities include lots of counting and reading numerals, and we ask questions like, "How many are left over?"

Contents

Squares

Let's sing

The square song

To the tune of 'The Grand Old Duke of York', sing this song as you draw a square in the air:

"A square is shaped like this
Four corners and four sides
And every side is the same length
So it's just as tall as wide…"

Let's do

The 'squares table'

Ask the children to collect square things to put on the table. These could include flat or solid shapes.

What else could we put on our table?

Squares in the hall

Ask the children to lie down to form a square on the floor.

How many bodies will we need?

How will we know when we have made a square?

Let's hold hands and make a square.

Let's stand one behind the other and walk till our line makes a square.

all together

Let's investigate

What is a square?

Sort through a box of shapes with the children. Tell them to give 'thumbs up' if they think a shape is a square and 'thumbs down' if they think it's not a square. When the shapes are sorted, ask the children to look closely at the pile of shapes they think are squares.

What do you notice about these shapes? Are they all squares? How can you tell?

What do they notice about the shapes in the other pile?

Square hunt

Walk round with the children, indoors and outside, looking for squares. Take some photographs of the children standing next to squares to make a 'Book of Squares'.

Can you find any squares? Where are they? What are they?

Squares at home

Encourage the children to look for squares at home, then come and tell the class about them tomorrow.

Ask a grown-up to help you look.

What is the smallest square you found? The biggest?

- masking tape
- a dice showing a different shape on each face
- plastic shapes
- a CD or cassette player

find

shape

circle

triangle

square

rectangle

in

inside

out

outside

different

all

Maths learning

Count reliably up to ten everyday objects

Use language to describe the shape and size of flat shapes

Use everyday words to describe position, direction and movement

Hop in a shape

Make large outlines of different shapes with masking tape, in the hall or outside area. Play some music and ask the children to walk or dance around. When the music stops the children have to run to a shape and hop in and out of it three times.

Things to ask

- What shape did you hop in?
- Can you hop in a square and then in another shape?
- This time, can you hop in any shape that isn't a square?
- Now find a friend and when the music stops hop in every square.

Challenges

Use a 'shape dice' and call out a particular shape for the children to hop in.

A child chooses a plastic shape, and must jump in a matching shape when the music stops.

Can the child...

Count the number of hops?

Identify and find a square to jump in?

Identify shapes that are not squares?

Approach new activities with confidence?

76

Dinosaur houses

Provide the children with a range of differently shaped construction material. Ask the children to make houses for a dinosaur family. Each child must be ready to explain to everyone how many dinosaurs could live in his house, and what shapes he used to make the house.

Things to ask

- Why did you choose to build your house out of Polydron?
- Which shapes will you use to build your house?
- How many dinosaurs can live in your house?
- Can you explain how you built your house? What did you do first?

Challenges

Child draw plans of their dinosaur houses.

Children extend their buildings to house more dinosaurs.

Can the child...

Use the language of shape to describe his building?

Count the number of dinosaurs in the house?

Talk about the construction of his house?

Carry out the activity independently?

Thread a square

* straws of various lengths
* weaving needles and thread

shape

square

edge

side

corner

straight

larger

how many?

count

one, two...

ask the children to choose either four or eight straws of the same length, and thread them together. Each child ties the ends of her thread to make her straws into a square. The children can then experiment with different lengths of straw, to make squares of different sizes.

Things to ask

* How many straws did you need to make your square?
* Sam used four straws to make his square, and Nadim used eight. What do you notice about these two squares?
* Could you make a bigger square?
* Could you make a smaller square?

Challenges

The children suspend the squares from a hoop to make a mobile.

Ask a child to make a square using twelve straws.

Can the child...

Count out the right number of straws?

Talk about some properties of squares, such as the number of edges or corners?

Compare one square with another square and recognise similarities?

Show curiosity and observation skills by talking about shapes?

Maths learning

Say and use the number names in order in familiar contexts

Count reliably up to ten everyday objects

Use language to describe the shape and size of flat shapes

Cubes in the bag

You will need
- a cloth bag, such as a pencil case, containing six cubes
- paper bags
- cubes
- Post–It notes
- felt-tipped pens

Give the children a bag containing six cubes. Can they find out how many cubes are in the bag by feeling? Open the bag and count the cubes together. As you put them back into the bag, count aloud and discuss how many cubes there would be if you put one more in the bag.

Invite the children to make and label paper bags of one, two, three, four and five cubes. Discuss what happens when they put one more cube in each bag.

Things to ask

- How many cubes do you think are in the bag?
- Why do you think there are that number of cubes?
- How can you work out how many cubes there will be if you put another one in the bag?
- How will you remember which bag has three (or four, or five) cubes in it?

Challenges

Children use Post-It notes to make labels for the bags showing the results of putting in one more cube.

Ask a child to find out what happens when he takes a cube out of a bag.

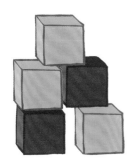

Can the child...

Count the cubes by touch and say how many?

Know what happens when a cube is added?

Use the words such as 'more than' and 'fewer than' when talking about numbers?

Maintain attention throughout the activity?

how many?
count
one, two...
one more
more than
less than
join in
tell me

Maths learning
Use language to compare two numbers
Count reliably up to ten everyday objects
Find one more or less than a number from 1 to 10

- cube-shaped boxes (not too large)
- a craft knife
- small objects such as beads, plastic elephants, bears, coins...

square

hollow

each

line

edge

corner

fit

how many?

one, two...

Maths learning

Count reliably up to ten everyday objects

Use language to describe the shape and size of flat shapes

Use everyday words to describe position

Fill in a square

Use a craft knife to cut some cube-shaped boxes into 'slices'. Give each pair of children a 'slice' to lay on the table. Then ask the children to choose some objects to put inside their square. Discuss the number of objects they are likely to be able to fit in if they fill the square, and suggest they try a range of different objects.

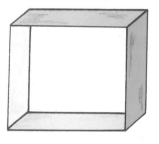
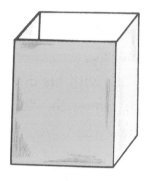
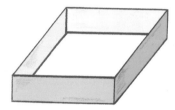

Things to ask

- Do you know the name of this shape [show the cube slice]?
- How many sides has your shape got? How many corners?
- How many elephants do you think will fit inside your square?
- Why do you think you will fit more beads than elephants inside your square?

Challenges

A pair of children find the greatest and least number of objects that will fit into their cube slice.

Children use slices of other boxes, of different shapes.

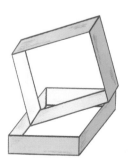

Can the child...

Use the language of shape?

Count reliably up to ten objects?

Use words such as 'more' or 'less' when making comparisons?

Select resources independently?

Dinosaur eggs

rrange twelve square pieces of paper on the table to make a square track. Ask the children to put out a 'dinosaur egg' (plastic shape) on each piece of paper. Establish a starting point, then each child takes a turn to roll the dice and count along the track with his dinosaur. He leaves the dinosaur where he lands, and picks up the 'egg' on the square. The children keep going round the track until all the 'eggs' have been collected.

You will need

- a dice marked '1, 1, 2, 2, 3, 3'
- a set of different 3D plastic shapes for the 'dinosaur eggs'
- plastic dinosaurs to use as counters
- small paper squares

Things to ask

- What number did you roll on the dice?
- How many shapes did you collect?
- Did you collect any cubes?
- How can you find out which shape you collected most of?

Challenges

Make the track longer and ask the children to collect more shapes.

Children use a number dice marked '1, 2, 3, 4, 5, 6'.

number

how many?

count

one, two...

shape

cube

cone

triangle

collect

Can the child...

Identify any of the shapes he has collected?

Read and say the numerals on the dice?

Count accurately round the number track?

Work cooperatively and take turns?

Maths learning

Count reliably up to ten everyday objects

Recognise numerals 1 to 9

Use language to describe the shape and size of solids

square

line

straight

edge

in

inside

repeat

continue

how many?

count

one, two...

Square in a square

sk each child to draw a big square, then draw another square inside that one, and another square inside that one... until she cannot fit any more.

The children count up how many squares they have drawn.

Things to ask

- How many squares do you think you will fit in? Guess before you try.
- Lauren has drawn each square in a different colour. How will that help her count?
- What can you do to help you count your squares? What can you do to remember the number you have got up to?
- Matteo tried using a larger piece of paper, but he made fewer squares than last time. Can you see why?

Challenges

Ask the children to draw a different pattern in each of the regions between the squares.

The children stick different items, such as pasta or tissue paper, in each region.

Can the child...

Estimate how many squares she will fit in her first square?

Have a strategy for counting the squares?

Use words such as 'inside' and 'next to' to describe her drawing?

Carry out the task independently?

Four makes a square

Players take turns to roll the dice, say the number, and pick up that many sticks. When a player has four sticks he can build a square. The winner is the first player to make four squares.

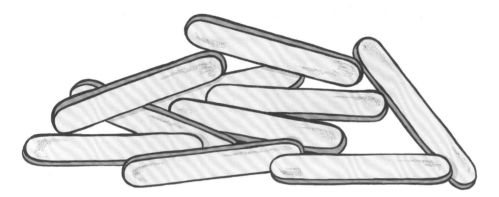

Things to ask

- You've got five sticks. Can you build a square yet?

- You've made your four squares. How many sticks do you have left over?

- How many sticks have you won altogether?

- Why do you think this game is called 'Four makes a square'? What do you think it would be called if you were making triangles? Or hexagons?

Challenges

Set a larger number of squares for the children to make.

A child makes a different shape: triangle, hexagon, pentagon, rectangle…

Can the child...

Organise his own collection of squares?

Count sticks and squares accurately?

Recognise when four squares have been completed?

Play the game taking turns and sharing cooperatively?

You will need

- dice marked with 1–3 spots
- sticks (such as matchsticks or lolly sticks)

square

how many?

count

one, two...

add

altogether

total

enough

more than

how many more?

Maths learning

Count reliably up to ten everyday objects

Begin to use the vocabulary involved in adding and subtracting

Use language to describe the shape and size of flat shapes

whole

part

apart

next to

square

side

corner

edge

straight

curved

Maths learning

Talk about, recognise and recreate simple patterns

Use developing mathematical ideas and methods to solve practical problems

Use language to describe the shape and size of flat shapes

Explode a square

Give each child a square of sticky paper and tell her to 'explode' it on to the sugar paper square. To do this, she cuts the sticky square into pieces and arranges these in any way she likes on the sugar paper — the only rule is she must use every bit of the original square.

Things to ask

- Would it be easy or hard to put your square back together? Why?
- Can you tell me about your exploded square?
- Can you remember what your square looked like, and how big it was, before you cut it up? Show me with your hands.
- How did Jade manage to get so many pieces from her square?

Challenges

Explode another square but make the result look different from last time.

Ask the children to choose their own shapes to 'explode'.

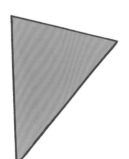

Can the child...

Use all the parts of her square without losing any?

Show an awareness that the amount of sticky paper has stayed the same?

Talk sensibly about what has happened to the square?

Arrange and stick the pieces confidently?

Put down a cube

Show the children the number track and discuss the numbers that they recognise. Then let the children take turns to roll the dice, count along the number track and put down a cube. Each child counts on from the previous cube without removing it. When the count reaches the end of the track, the children read out the numbers that are not covered by a cube.

Things to ask

- What number did you roll on the dice?
- How will you remember where the last turn ended?
- If you have to jump on two squares from 7, what number will you land on?
- How many numbers on our track aren't covered by a cube?

Challenges

Invite the children to play the game again and see how many numbers they cover this time.

Children make a record of the numbers that do not have a cube on them.

Can the child...

Recognise the number pattern on the dice?

Count the right number along the track?

Recognise some of the numerals on the track?

Work cooperatively in a group?

You will need

- a 0–20 number track
- an ordinary 1–6 dice
- square counters or cubes

how many?

count

one, two...

same number

different number

number track

put

place

Maths learning

Count reliably up to ten everyday objects

Recognise numerals 1 to 9

Use developing mathematical ideas and methods to solve practical problems

Numbers in a square

how many?

count

one, two...

altogether

square

corner

arrange

rearrange

same way

different way

Give each child a square of paper and ten plastic bears. Ask the children to arrange their bears by the corners of the squares. Discuss the different arrangements they make.

Then ask the children to gather their bears at the centre of the paper and count them. Encourage the children to make new arrangements of bears at the corners of the square, gathering and counting them each time. Suggest they try this several times.

Things to ask

● How many bears have you got altogether?
● Can you explain how you arranged your bears?
● Can you think of another way to arrange your bears?
● How can you remember what you've done?

Challenges

Children choose a different number of bears to arrange.

Children choose different shapes of paper.

Can the child...

Count accurately her collection of bears?

Arrange all her bears into the corners of the square?

Reorganise her bears into a new arrangement?

Talk about what she is doing?

Boxes

Draw a 4 × 5 grid of dots on the board. Take turns with the children to join two dots with the aim of making boxes. When you complete a box, write your initial in it. When a child completes a box, he draws a smiley face in it.

When the whole grid has been made into boxes, count up how many boxes you and the children have made. The side with the most boxes is the winner.

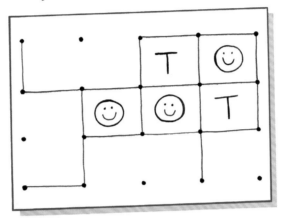

Things to ask

- How many lines does a box need?
- How many lines do you need to make two boxes side by side? Let's count them: one, two…
- Lukas has made two boxes in one go. How did he do it?
- When you play this game with a friend, what will you write/draw in your boxes to show they are yours?

Challenges

The children play this game in pairs on dotted paper grids, and take grids home to play with their grown-ups.

Children make their own dotted grids.

Understand how to play the game?

Play the game cooperatively with a partner?

Draw the squares accurately?

Actively take part in the whole class game?

you will need
- dotted grids
- pencils and felt-tipped pens

square

join

line

straight

side

up

down

how many?

one, two…

more

fewer

Maths learning
Count reliably up to ten everyday objects

Use developing mathematical ideas and methods to solve practical problems

Use everyday words to describe position

Planning and assessment

The mathematics covered in Squares

Learning goal	Boxes	Numbers in a square	Put down a cube	Explode a square	Four makes a square	Square in a square	Dinosaur eggs	Fill in a square	Cubes in the bag	Thread a square	Dinosaur houses	Hop in a shape
Numbers (as labels and for counting)												
use some number names and number language	★	★	★	★	★	★	★	★	★	★	★	★
count with some numbers in the correct order	★	★	★	★	★	★	★	★	★	★	★	★
recognise groups with one, two or three objects	★	★	★		★	★	★	★	★	★	★	
count up to four objects by saying one number name for each	★	★	★	★	★	★	★	★	★	★	★	
represent numbers using fingers, pictures or marks on paper						★	★	★				
recognise numerals up to 9			★			★	★	★			★	
count out up to six objects from a larger group	★	★			★		★	★	★	★		
count up to or beyond ten objects	★	★	★		★	★	★	★	★	★	★	
Numbers (for calculating)												
compare two groups of objects and say when the groups are equal in number		★	★			★	★	★		★		
find the total number of items in two groups by counting all of them					★					★		
predict how many objects will be left when one or two are taken away			★		★				★	★		★
say the number that is one more than a given number					★					★		
Shape and space												
use positional language to describe location and movement	★					★	★	★		★	★	★
select and use shapes appropriately for a given task	★	★		★	★	★	★	★		★	★	★
choose to match similar shapes										★		
describe a simple journey												★
select an example of a named shape	★	★	★	★	★	★	★	★	★	★	★	★
show awareness of symmetry	★			★	★						★	
find 2D and 3D shapes that will fit together						★					★	
Measures												
use measuring language such as 'high', 'short', 'heavy' and words to describe time		★			★	★	★	★	★		★	★
talk about instruments we can use for measuring, such as hands and scales												
order two or three items by length, height, weight or capacity				★								

Dough

Modelling dough offers all kinds of opportunities to investigate size, weight and shape. We can make and talk about 2D and 3D shapes, and strengthen our reading by making numerals out of dough. We break a large dough ball into smaller balls to explore how the number of balls changes with the size we make them, use our sense of touch to estimate and compare weights, and make longer caterpillars by using more balls or bigger balls.

We also practise adding and counting in twos.

Contents

Dough

Let's sing

s s s s

"Ten fat sausages"

Sing with the class:

"Ten fat sausages sizzling in the pan;
  One went POP!
  And another went BANG!"

Make 'sausages' from dough so that you can enact the song as you go along.

What other songs could we make dough props for? Let's try one out.

Let's do

"Which is missing?"

Make five balls of dough and lay them in a row. Count them with the children and talk about how many there are altogether. Then remove one ball from the row.

How many balls are there now?

If I take away two balls, can you tell me how many there will be in the line?

"From a ball of dough I could make..."

Encourage the children to imagine and share all the different things they think they could make out of a ball of dough: a snake, letter, boat, numeral…

How many different things can you think of? How can we remember all these different ideas?

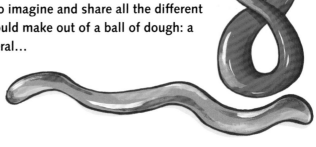

all together

Let's investigate

Shapes

Hold up a plastic or wooden triangle so that all the children can see it.

If I put a blob of dough on each corner, how many blobs would I need?

What about a square? A rectangle? A hexagon? A circle?

How can we check our answers?

"What's bigger?"

Make a ball of dough and show it to the children. Ask everyone to find something in the room that is bigger than the ball. Encourage the children to share and discuss their ideas. Then ask each child to show his objects and compare them with the ball of dough.

Can you think of something that is smaller than the ball?

Can you think of something about the same size as the ball?

- wooden numerals or number cards
- dough
- rolling pins

zero

one, two...

number

straight

curved

left

right

read

match

Number roll

ask the children to make some numbers with dough. You can use wooden numerals or number cards to model the numbers the children make. Show each child how to roll a long snake of dough and shape it to make her number. She could use a rolling pin to flatten the dough. When a child's number is ready, she can ask a friend to guess what the number is.

Things to ask

- Can you make the number of your street door? Your age? Your phone number?
- Which numbers are made from curved lines? And which are all straight lines? Which have mixture of both?
- How can you tell if your '3' is round the right way?
- How do you know Reena has made a '2'?

Challenges

Invite the child to find a wooden numeral to match her dough numeral.

Challenge a child to make the highest number she can from the completed dough numerals.

Can the child...

Recognise and name some numbers?

Make a good attempt at shaping the numbers with dough?

Say when a number is the wrong way round or is like another shape?

Show a high level of involvement in the activity?

Maths learning

Say and use the number names in order in familiar contexts

Recognise numerals 1 to 9

Use language to describe the shape and size of solids and flat shapes

Caterpillar count

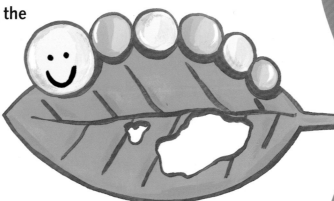

Show the children how to make a caterpillar by rolling the dough up into small balls and pushing these together. Invite the children to make their own caterpillars of all different lengths.

Things to ask

● Which of your caterpillars is made with the most or fewest balls?

● This caterpillar is made of four balls. How many would there be if I added one more ball?

● This caterpillar is made of six balls. Would a caterpillar made of three balls be longer or shorter? What do you think?

● How many balls of dough would you need to make a really, really long caterpillar?

Challenges

Children toss a dice and add on that many balls to their caterpillars. The game ends when a target number is reached.

Challenge a child to make a caterpillar the length of the table.

Can the child...

Compare two caterpillars and say which is made of more or fewer balls, or whether they have the same number?

Compare two caterpillars and say which is the longest or shortest, or whether they are about the same length?

Talk about what will happen if he puts two caterpillars together?

Make a caterpillar independently?

Dough

You will need
● dough

how many?

the same number as

one more

longer

longest

shorter

shortest

more

most

fewer

fewest

Maths learning
Find one more or less than a number from 1 to 10

Begin to relate addition to combining two groups of objects

Use language to compare two quantities

93

Dough

guess

estimate

check

balance

scales

measure

weigh

heavier

heaviest

lighter

lightest

Maths learning

Use developing mathematical ideas and methods to solve practical problems

Use language to compare two quantities

Use language to describe the size of solids

94

Balance

@sk each child to make a dough ball. The children work in pairs to find out whose ball is heavier — or whether they weigh about the same.

The children continue the activity, making new dough balls and weighing them.

Things to ask

- Hold a ball in each hand. Which hand feels like it wants to go down more?

- Put a ball in each bucket of the bucket scales. Which side goes down more? And what does that mean?

- Rohan's ball is lighter than Dominic's. How could he make it heavier?

- Jinan's ball is heavier than Kimala's. What can they do to make them weigh about the same?

Challenges

A child makes three or four balls, all of different weights.

Children make two balls that weigh the same.

Can the child...

Understand how to use his hands to compare weights?

Use bucket scales appropriately to compare weights?

Demonstrate how to make a ball of dough that is heavier than, lighter than or about the same weight as another?

Talk about what she is doing?

Hedgehog

Invite the children to prepare several round balls of dough, and cut these in half. Each child starts the game with one half. The players take turns to roll the dice and collect spines (straws) for their hedgehogs. When a player's first hedgehog has five spines, he begins a new one. The winner is the first player to complete five hedgehogs.

Things to ask

● If you throw a 0, how many matchsticks can you pick up?

● How many hedgehogs did you make?

● How many hedgehogs can you make with ten matchsticks?

● Fadi has thrown a 3. He only needs one spine to finish his first hedgehog; what's he going to do with the other spines?

Challenges

Give the children a 1–6 dice; each hedgehog can still only have five spines.

Children try to work out how many matchsticks are needed to win, and if this number is always the same.

Can the child...

Recognise the numerals on the dice and collect that many sticks?

Know what to do when the target number is reached on each hedgehog?

Count accurately and continue the count from one hedgehog to the next?

Work cooperatively as part of a group?

You will need

● balls of dough
● cutting tools
● short lengths cut from straws, or matchsticks
● a dice marked '0, 1, 2, 2, 3, 3'

zero

one, two...

how many?

count

add up

altogether

enough

not enough

how many are left over?

how many more?

Maths learning

Count reliably up to ten everyday objects

Recognise numerals 1 to 9

Begin to relate addition to combining two groups of objects

You will need

- a 1–3 dice
- a sand timer
- a small slab of dough and a stick for each player

how many?

guess

count

more than

greater than

about the same as

most

fewer than

fewest

compare

The dotty game

Start the timer. Each player takes a turn to roll the dice and record that number in her dough, by marking that number of dots with the end of her stick. The game ends when the sand has run through. Players then discuss who made the most dots.

Things to ask

- Who do you guess has most dots? Why do you think that?

- How many dots did you make?

- Was your guess close to the correct number or far away? Let's look at the numbers on a number line and see if they are close together.

- How did you count the dots? What can make counting them easier?

Challenges

Give the children a 1–6 dice or a timer that takes longer to run through.

A child counts someone else's dough dots.

Can the child...

Make the correct number of dots each time?

Recount to find the total number of dots?

Identify who has the most or fewest dots?

Play the game independently and cooperatively?

Draw and make

sk each child to draw a shape on paper. Then the child tries to make his shape again, with dough. Invite the children to discuss their ideas about how to do this.

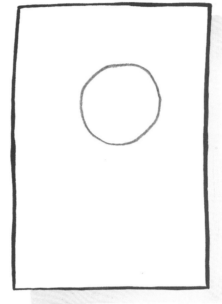

copy

make

same

different

describe

shape

corner

round

curved

straight

Things to ask

● Describe your drawing to me. Now tell me about the dough shape. How are they the same? And how are they different?

● Was your dough shape easy or hard to make? Why?

● Draw a shape for someone else to make.

● What other things can you draw and then try to make in dough?

Challenges

Children make flat shapes from dough, and then draw them.

A child chooses a shape from the box of solids (or building blocks) and tries to make a duplicate from dough.

Can the child...

Draw something that is possible to make?

Make a close representation of the drawn shape?

Compare and talk about the drawn and the made shape?

Carry out the activity independently?

Maths learning

Use developing mathematical ideas and methods to solve practical problems

Use language to describe the shape and size of solids and flat shapes

Use everyday words to describe position

how many?

count

one, two...

same number

one more

in order

match

make

Bread rolls

sk each child to make a set of six 'bread rolls' using dough. Show them how to make a row of dots on the top of each roll so that the first roll has one dot, the second has two dots, and so on up to six dots.

Then put the rolls in the centre of the table and play the 'Bread Roll Game'. The children take turns to throw the dice and find the roll with that many dots. The winner is the first to collect three rolls with the same number of dots.

Things to ask

● How many dots do you need to make on that roll?

● How can you check that you've make a set of rolls with dots from one to six?

● Can you explain how to play the game?

● What have you decided to collect?

Challenges

Children try collecting six rolls in order.

Children make rolls with up to ten dots and play the game using a 1–10 number spinner.

Maths learning

Say and use the number names in order in familiar contexts

Count reliably up to ten everyday objects

Use developing mathematical ideas and methods to solve practical problems

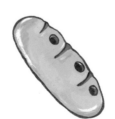

Can the child...

Work systematically to make a set of bread rolls?

Put the rolls in order?

Recognise patterns on the dice?

Take turns when playing a game?

From one ball

sk each child to make a dough ball and then find out how many small balls he can make from it. When the children have finished, ask them to make all the small balls back into one large ball and repeat the activity. This time each child should try to make more balls.

how many?

estimate

guess

count

number

one, two...

more than

fewer than

compare

Things to ask

● Guess how many balls you have made before you count.

● How many balls did you make altogether?

● How can you make sure you make more balls this time?

● What can you do to remember the number of balls you make each time?

Challenges

The children try to make fewer balls than last time.

Set a target number of small balls for the children to make from the large ball.

Can the child...

Make a reasonable estimate of how many little balls he has made?

Compare two numbers and work out which is more?

Think of a way to record what he has made?

Carry out the activity independently?

Maths learning

Say and use the number names in order in familiar contexts

Count reliably up to ten everyday objects

Use developing mathematical ideas and methods to solve practical problems

- dough
- sticks
- paints or ink pads
- paper

how many?

count

number

one, two...

one more,
two more...

find out

work out

altogether

total

Lots of dots

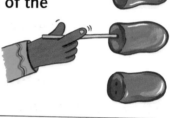

Show the children how to roll a fat cylindrical shape of dough and flatten one end of the cylinder on the table to make a printing pad. The children make dotty holes in their printing pads by carefully pushing a stick into the dough, and count how many holes they have made.

Each child can make a series of prints on paper with her dough printing pad. When the work is dry ask each child to guess, then find out, how many dots she has printed.

Things to ask

- How many dots are on your printing pad?
- How many dots did you print altogether? Count with me: one, two…
- Jason's printing pad has two dots. Let's count the dots Jason printed in twos: two, four…
- How can we remember which dots we have already counted?

Challenges

A child makes two holes in her pad, and prints ten dots.

The children use their printing pads to print a dotty number line.

Can the child...

Count the number of dots on the printing pad?

Explain what is happening to the number of dots each time she prints?

Count the printed dots in ones? In twos?

Work cooperatively in a group situation?

Maths learning

Count reliably up to ten everyday objects

Begin to relate addition to combining two groups of objects

Talk about, recognise and recreate simple patterns

Frame it

ask each child to draw a picture in the centre of a small piece of card. Then invite the children to make dough frames to fit around the edges of the cards. The frames can be stuck on with ordinary classroom glue.

Invite the children to show each other, and talk about, the various patterns and designs they have made.

Things to ask

● How can you make sure that the frame fits the card?

● What could you use to decorate your frame?

● What shape is your picture?

● How many pieces of dough did you use to make your frame?

Challenges

Children make different frames to fit pictures of all shapes and sizes.

A child makes a frame to look through, and describes what he can see.

Can the child...

Work systematically and complete the task?

Ensure that the frame fits all the way around the edge?

Think of other shapes to try out and act upon his ideas?

Talk about what he is doing?

You will need

● card
● pencils, crayons and felt-tipped pens
● dough
● dough cutters
● sticks
● glue

edge

enough

shape

triangle

rectangle

pattern

top

bottom

curved

straight

Maths learning

Talk about, recognise and recreate simple patterns

Use language to describe the shape and size of solids and flat shapes

Use everyday words to describe position and direction

You will need

● dough
● a dice marked
  '0, 1, 2, 2, 3, 3'
● a plastic container
  to be the
  'snake pit'

how many?

one, two...

longer

longest

shorter

shortest

start from

across

choose

best way

Maths learning

Count reliably up to ten
everyday objects

Recognise numerals 1 to 9

Use language to compare
two quantities

Snakes

sk the children to make snakes of all different sizes out of dough, and put them in the 'snake pit'. Chalk a start line and a finish line on the table.

Each player takes a turn to roll the dice and read out the number; she chooses that many snakes from the pit and places them end to end, to make a line from the start. The game ends when one player's line reaches the finish, or there are no more snakes. The winner is the player who reached the finish, or had the longest line when the snakes ran out.

Things to ask

● Which snakes are you going to choose?

● How did you get across so quickly?

● How many snakes were left over at the end of the game?

● Did you make enough snakes to get right across the table?

Challenges

Change the rules so that the winner is the person with the shortest line.

The children play so that the person with the most snakes is the winner.

Can the child...

Recognise the dice numerals?

Consider length when choosing snakes?

Talk about her decision-making process?

Tell someone else how to play the game?

Ladybird sparkles

ask the children to make ladybirds from pieces of red dough. They can use sticks to draw a line down the middle of the dough, to show the wings. Then suggest that the children use sequins to give the ladybird some spots.

Talk to the children about the different arrangements of spots they are making.

You will need

- dough, coloured red
- sequins
- small sticks, such as tooth picks

how many?

one, two...

investigate

same

different

add

count on

altogether

makes

symmetrical

Things to ask

- How many spots does your ladybird have?
- Can you make a ladybird that has the same number of spots on each side?
- Count the spots. Can you find those numbers on the number line?
- Can you find a ladybird with five spots?

Challenges

Ask a child to make a ladybird with a particular number of spots.

Make a 'sparkly spots' number line with the children, by putting the ladybirds in order to show one of each number of spots.

Can the child...

Talk about number doubles?

Make a symmetrical ladybird?

Count the spots on each side of the ladybird and count the total of spots?

Persist with the activity for an extended period of time?

Maths learning

Count reliably up to ten everyday objects

Begin to relate addition to combining two groups of objects

Talk about, recognise and recreate simple patterns

103

Planning and assessment

The mathematics covered in Dough

Significant steps leading to the Early Learning Goals	Number roll	Caterpillar count	Balance	Hedgehog	The dotty game	Draw and make	Bread rolls	From one ball	Lots of dots	Frame it	Snakes	Ladybird sparkles
Numbers (as labels and for counting)												
use some number names and number language	★	★		★	★		★	★	★		★	★
count with some numbers in the correct order		★		★	★		★	★	★		★	★
recognise groups with one, two or three objects		★			★			★	★			★
count up to four objects by saying one number name for each				★			★	★			★	★
represent numbers using fingers, pictures or marks on paper	★											
recognise numerals up to 9												
count out up to six objects from a larger group				★							★	
count up to or beyond ten objects		★		★	★		★	★	★		★	★
Numbers (for calculating)												
compare two groups of objects and say when the groups are equal in number		★		★			★	★	★		★	★
find the total number of items in two groups by counting all of them		★			★				★			★
predict how many objects will be left when one or two are taken away				★			★					
say the number that is one more than a given number												
Shape and space												
use positional language to describe location and movement	★	★								★		
select and use shapes appropriately for a given task			★			★				★		★
choose to match similar shapes	★					★				★		
describe a simple journey												
select an example of a named shape	★					★				★		
show awareness of symmetry						★			★	★		★
find 2D and 3D shapes that will fit together												
Measures												
use measuring language such as 'high', 'short', 'heavy' and words to describe time		★	★					★		★	★	
talk about instruments we can use for measuring, such as hands and scales			★		★						★	
order two or three items by length, height, weight or capacity		★	★								★	

Further reading

*Learning Mathematics in the Nursery:
Desirable Approaches*
the Early Childhood Mathematics Group
BEAM Education 1997

*Extending Thought in Young Children:
A Parent-Teacher Partnership*
C Athey
Paul Chapman 1990

*Mathematics for Young Children:
An Active Thinking Approach*
M H Bird
Routledge 1991

*Mathematical Beginnings:
Problem Solving for Young Children*
J Blinko and N Graham
Claire Publications 1988

*Exploring Mathematics with Younger
Children*
(an ATM Activity Book)
Association of Teachers of Mathematics
1991

Number in the Nursery and Reception
Sue Gifford with Patti Barber and
Sheila Ebbutt
BEAM Education 1998

*Teaching Numeracy:
Maths in the Primary Classroom*
edited by Ruth Merttens
Scholastic 1996

*Teaching Mathematics to Young
Children: 4–7*
C Mitchell and H Williams
Chris Kington Publishing 1998

*Nursery Mathematics:
A Development for 3–5 Year Olds*
Heinemann Maths Plus 1997

*Supporting Mathematical Development
in the Early Years*
L Pound
Oxford University Press 1999

Teaching and Learning Early Number
edited by I Thompson
Oxford University Press 1997

Teaching the Early Years
H Williams, C Skinner and P Barber
Rigby 2000

Early learning goals	Hands												Containers												Teddy				
	Hand prints	Gloves	Feelies	On your hand	Hide it	Clap hands	A handful	Touchy	Finger prints	Measuring with hands	Finger counting	Hide and seek	Inside, inside, inside	Fill it up	Bubble box	Change it	Flower pots	Box wrap	Sink the boat	Container counts	The 'same as' game	Pirate's treasure	One to one	Lids on!	Put the bear to bed	All sorts	What will bear wear?	Lead the way	Bear hunt
Say and use the number names in order in familiar contexts	★	★	★	★	★	★	★	★	★	★	★	★		★	★		★	★	★	★	★	★	★				★		★
Count reliably up to ten everyday objects		★	★	★	★	★	★	★	★	★	★	★		★	★		★	★	★	★	★	★	★				★		★
Recognise numerals 1 to 9					★				★					★			★						★						
Use language to compare two numbers						★			★		★	★						★		★	★	★							
Begin to use the vocabulary involved in adding and subtracting			★								★																		
Find one more or less than a number from 1 to 10		★				★					★								★										
Begin to relate addition to combining two groups of objects											★										★								
Begin to relate subtraction to 'taking away'											★											★							
Talk about, recognise and recreate simple patterns		★						★																		★	★	★	
Use developing mathematical ideas and methods to solve practical problems	★	★		★		★	★		★		★	★	★	★	★	★	★	★	★	★		★	★		★	★	★	★	★
Use language to compare two quantities			★	★	★		★		★	★	★	★	★	★	★	★		★	★	★	★	★	★	★					
Use language to describe the shape and size of solids and flat shapes			★						★				★		★	★		★		★		★		★	★	★	★		
Use everyday words to describe position, direction and movement	★					★							★		★		★								★	★		★	★

Planning and assessment

This chart cross-references the activities in MiniMaths to the Early Learning Goals. These are identified by the QCA (Qualifications and Curriculum Authority) as the levels of attainment that children should have reached by the end of their Reception year. For more detailed assessment of the significant steps leading to the Early Learning Goals, please refer to the chart at the end of each chapter.

	bears								Green peppers											Squares												Dough											
	In the bears' house	Doubles	All in order	My bear	Compare the bear	Bears in a bus queue	How many missing?	Make a mistake	Print a red pepper	Apple stars	Green things	Market stall	Salad day	Green... not green	Peas in a pod	I like green peppers	Five on a plate	Get the dinner ready	Ugh — yuck!	Hop in a shape	Dinosaur houses	Thread a square	Cubes in the bag	Fill in a square	Dinosaur eggs	Square in a square	Four makes a square	Explode a square	Put down a cube	Numbers in a square	Boxes	Number roll	Caterpillar count	Balance	Hedgehog	The dotty game	Draw and make	Bread rolls	From one ball	Lots of dots	Frame it	Snakes	Ladybird sparkles
		★		★		★	★				★	★	★	★	★	★	★	★	★	★	★	★	★	★	★	★	★		★	★	★	★	★		★	★		★	★	★		★	★
	★	★		★		★	★			★	★	★	★	★	★	★	★	★	★	★	★	★	★	★	★	★	★		★	★	★		★		★	★		★	★	★		★	★
	★					★						★			★								★			★			★			★			★				★			★	
		★				★	★				★			★	★	★	★		★			★	★		★	★			★			★		★			★					★	
	★					★	★				★				★								★			★			★			★		★								★	
															★																	★											
	★	★				★	★				★			★			★						★			★			★		★			★	★			★					★
							★				★																					★											
					★	★	★																						★		★	★				★			★	★		★	
	★		★	★	★	★	★	★	★	★	★	★		★			★	★	★	★	★	★	★		★		★	★	★	★	★	★	★		★	★	★	★	★			★	★
		★	★						★	★	★	★	★		★	★			★		★	★	★		★	★	★		★	★		★	★	★	★			★				★	★
			★	★	★			★		★	★		★						★	★	★		★	★		★	★		★	★	★	★	★	★		★			★			★	★
			★	★				★	★	★	★							★		★	★	★		★		★		★		★	★							★				★	★

Our thanks to...

Besime Altintas, Funda Elâgöz, Yeser Tonyel and The Future American Elementary School, Cyprus

Christine Ames and Edenthorpe Hall Primary School, Doncaster

Helen Andrews and Reed First School, Royston, Hertfordshire

Mark Bartlett and the Professional Education Centre, Pembrokeshire

Radka Benton and Radley CE Primary School, Abingdon

Susan Bostock and Warton Nethersoles CE Primary School, Staffordshire

Anne Brouard and Hautes Capelles Infant School, Guernsey

Anne-Marie Buchanan, Caroline Foster and Lyndhurst Primary School, London

Barbara Carr and Cranford House School, Moulsford, Oxfordshire

Muriel Chester and the Southwark BEAM Group

Carol Chesters and St Nicholas House Nursery, Hemel Hempstead

Jinty Christian and Longniddry Primary School, East Lothian

Peter Clarke, Primary Mathematics Advisor

Shelagh Cosgrow and St Ursula's Infant School, Romford, Essex

Marion Cranmer and Dog Kennel Hill Primary School, London

Diane Crotcher, Gaynor Walker and Miers Court Primary School, Rainham, Kent

Maria Dean and Hawsey CP School, Cooksbridge, East Sussex

Claire Degenkolb and Hall Green Nursery, Birmingham

Ruth Duckworth, Janet Ellis and Sowerby CP School, North Yorkshire

John Ellard and Wellsmead First School, Milton Keynes

Huw Evans and Herdings JNI School, Sheffield

Sally Ewbank, Helen Morrison and Kilham CE Infant School, East Yorkshire

Barbara Ford, Bev Green, Diane Hargreaves and Langworthy Road CP School, Salford

Sue Frazer and Milwards CP School, Harlow, Essex

Rosemary Hafeez and the Croydon BEAM Group

Ruth Hall and Slinfold CE Primary School, Horsham

Janice Hamilton and West Green Primary School, London

Helen Hancock and Patcham Infant School, Brighton

JE Harris and Henham & Ugley Primary School, Bishop's Stortford, Essex

Sue Harris and St Joseph's RC Primary School, Darlaston

Senga Harrison and St Jude's CE Primary School, London

Stephanie Hewison and Kirkoswald CE Primary School, Cumbria

Karen Holman and Long Buckby Junior School, Northamptonshire

Pauline Hopkins and Wyke Primary School, Gillingham, Dorset

Karen Johnston and Oxhey Infant School, Hertfordshire

Jilly Lake and Morgan House Kindergarten, Oxfordshire

Hilary Loder and The Meadow Special School, Middlesex

Liz Luck and Okehampton Primary School, Devon

Christine Lumb and Tyersal First School, Bradford

Joy Lynch and St George's Cathedral School, London

Adèle Markey and Bury & Whitefield Jewish Primary School, Lancashire

Margaret McCallion and Claregate Primary School, Wolverhampton

Ann McTegart, Sarah Rodda and St Aloysius RC Infant School, London

Vivienne Millward and Low Bentham CP School, Lancaster

Margaret Misson and Monks Orchard Primary School, Croydon

Nick Moon and The European School, Brussels, Belgium

Amanda Morgan and Malpas Church in Wales Infant School, Newport

Deborah Mottram, Jane Price and The Giffard RC Primary School, Wolverhampton

Sally Northcott and Maesglas Primary School, Newport

Jackie O'Callaghan and Gifford Primary School, London

Carol Palmer and Valley Road Infant School, Sunderland

Julie Plumstead and Bevendean Primary School, Brighton

Verena Powell and Wadhurst Primary School, East Sussex

Annie Owens, Independent Consultant

Jane Prothero and Grimes Dyke Primary School, Leeds

Susan Robinson and Webbers School, Holcombe Rogus

Helen Smith and The Holy Family RC Primary School, Surrey

Marguerite Sparks and Downsview Primary School, Croydon

Angela Stephenson and St Mary Magdalene's RC Primary School, Bexhill-on-Sea

Lis Stuart, Helen Tressler and Grange Infant School, Daventry

Ann Todd and Beech Street CP School, Manchester

Christine Walsh and St Chad's Nursery, Leeds

Aimée Warren and Bishop Warrington-Ingram School, Ruislip, Middlesex

Sue Webb, Gay Whent and Wood Ley CP School, Stowmarket, Suffolk

Susan Yates and Patcham House School, Brighton